December 1986

Merry Christmas Dad!
   Love,
      Kate

DIETRICH

DIETRICH

ALEXANDER WALKER

Illustrations from the Kobal Collection

1817

HARPER & ROW, PUBLISHERS, New York

Cambridge, Philadelphia, San Francisco,
London, Mexico City, São Paulo, Sydney

Frontispiece and opposite: Dietrich in 1932
(photos by E. R. Richee and Don English respectively).

First U.S. edition

Library of Congress Cataloging in Publication Data

Walker, Alexander.
  Dietrich.

  Bibliography: p.
  Filmography: p.
  Includes index.
  1. Dietrich, Marlene, 1904–   2. Entertainers—
German—Biography.   I. Title.
PN2658.D5W34   1984   791.43′028′0924 [B] 84-47607
ISBN 0-06-015319-9

84 85 86 87 88 10 9 8 7 6 5 4 3 2 1

CONTENTS

FOR BEATRIX MILLER

BERLIN

BERLIN

If truth is "the first casualty of war," then the first beneficiary is probably legend. Marlene Dietrich has been able to reap the rewards both ways. World War I and the chaos it produced concealed until quite recently some of the most basic facts about her origins and upbringing. And World War II, along with the part she played in it, served to magnify the unique constituents of a romantic legend that the cinema screen had already formed. Indeed, the concept of militarism has run throughout Marlene Dietrich's whole existence, public and private, factual and fictitious, shaping her growth, formulating her loyalties, annealing her image to an impregnable durability. She is an extraordinary anachronism because of this: no star of today, no female star anyhow, would dare to personify the romantic side of the warrior myth as Dietrich still does in image, words and person. It would take a war correspondent or a war photographer to portray the fighting man's virtues with the resonating emotion that this actress can convey with a look or a line of dialogue or a stance or the verse of a ballad.

Marlene Dietrich releases a feeling about the romantic myth of war which we should find unpalatable, to say the least, if it were associated with anyone who did not come out of an era when war was regarded as something gallant and honorable and just—provided that the men who fought it, and the women who brought moral and sometimes physical comfort to those men, shared in such convictions. Dietrich once said with characteristic firmness: "I am a Prussian." The phrase vibrates as plangently in terms of a certain kind of outlook as that other commitment to a way of life spoken many years later in the city that was her birthplace by another possessor of a romantic myth—"I am a Berliner."

The purpose of biography is to assign meaning to a life. Marlene Dietrich's life is one that derives its meaning from the way in which a unique individual persuades us to see it refracted through the many facets of her personality and talents. One of her directors, Rouben Mamoulian, once revealed that he kept a book in which he invited his celebrated friends to write down their innermost thoughts. Dietrich wrote: "The most important thing in life is love, duty. The most important thing in work is beauty, discipline." It is an aphorism wholly characteristic of her own well-ordered Teutonic mind: it moderates her "Prussianism" with her "feminism," but puts the womanly virtues in partnership with the military imperatives.

8

At the same time, biography seeks to resolve the confusions of fact and truth that comprise a "life." In Dietrich's case, finding the facts is sometimes even more difficult than hazarding a reflection on what they mean in terms of myth. Many pertinent facts have been concealed or even destroyed by the circumstances of the same war that served so well to produce the myth. It comes as a shock, for instance, to realize that we actually know far less *for certain* about Dietrich than we do about her far more reclusive contemporary, Greta Garbo. For a very long time, indeed, even the date and place of Dietrich's birth depended upon which version of her life one read, including the lady's own various accounts of it. Her birth certificate had no doubt been filed away in the pigeonholes of Prussian thoroughness, but its exact location had been forgotten in the social confusion of two World Wars. If Dietrich herself possessed a copy of the document, she preferred not to display it but simply to quote a likely figure—"1904" was usually the year, "Weimar" or "Berlin" sometimes the place. Not until fairly recent times, in 1964 to be exact (since we are dealing with dates), did a clerk in East Berlin locate what he claimed to be Dietrich's birth certificate and, rather unsportingly, forward it to officials in West Berlin. Even less gallantly, they publicized the date on it: December 27, 1901. And the place: Berlin.

She was the younger daughter—by about a year—of Louis Erich Otto Dietrich and Wilhelmina Elisabeth Josephine Felsing. Some doubt persists about the father's status in the Prussian society of his time. True, he had been an officer in the crack Uhlan Cavalry and served with distinction in the Franco-Prussian War of 1870–71. His bravery in the field won him the Iron Cross and promotion to the rank of major. This should have set his future career firmly within the prestigious framework of his regiment: instead, he resigned from the army in 1883 or 1884, following his marriage to the daughter of a Berlin retailer. The firm of Conrad Felsing, at 20 Unter den Linden, had been founded in the nineteenth century, and a "Berliner Adressbuch" (directory) for the year 1905 testifies impressively to its range of stock, which included "Monumenten, Büsten und Statuetten in echter und Kunstbronze" and, perhaps more relevant to the engagement of the founder's granddaughter to a Prussian officer, "Infanterie—und Kavallerie—Statuetten für jedes Regiment des deutschen Heeres."

Now permission for someone of Major Dietrich's rank and distinction to marry was traditionally a matter reserved to the discretion of his commanding officer. "Good connections" preserved a regiment's exclusiveness quite as surely as the winning of battle honors established its traditions. Both were jealously guarded: "blood" was preferred to "trade" when the commanding officer's permission was sought. There can be little doubt that serving the aristocracy's taste in figurines and watches ("Garantie für jede Uhr drei Jahre!") would not have been as good a recommendation for a bride's background as actually *being* the aristocracy. Anyway, the marriage went ahead; presumably Major Dietrich preferred to forfeit his career rather than his bride. Upon resigning his commission in the Uhlans, he became a lieutenant in the Royal Prussian Police, a step down in

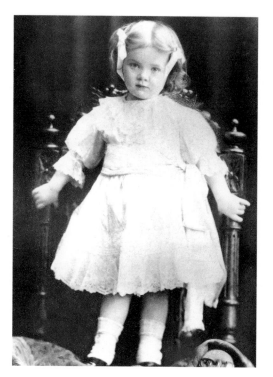

Maria Magdalene Dietrich,
aged respectively two and
five.

several ways, despite the rigorously paramilitary organization of the force. Dietrich's earliest memory of her father—indeed, virtually the only memory of him that she has made public—is still strongly impregnated with the sight, sound and even smell of military appurtenances: the smell of leather, the shine of his boots, the sound of a riding crop habitually slapping the leg of stiff serge breeches the color of a Victoria plum.

Dietrich's maternal grandfather, Conrad Felsing, had French connections: hence the "C" rather than the Teutonic "K" in his first name. Whether the family had also Jewish antecedents must remain speculative. But since a large part of the Berlin jewelry trade was in Jewish hands, as was (and is) the case in metropolitan cities the world over, Jewish business and social connections would have been a commonplace feature of Dietrich's early life. These may have played some unvoiced part in her later abhorrence of Nazi rule and her decision to follow her career outside Hitler's Germany, even though artists of enough distinction could be officially reclassified as Aryan, if they were ready to collude with the distasteful masquerade it involved. Dietrich's given names were Maria Magdalene; but, as if effecting a compromise between the heavy German syllables and her French antecedents, she eventually elided them into the lighter-toned "Marlene" and thus, with felicitous but quite unconscious effect, assisted Noël Coward, in his introduction to her Café de Paris act in London nearly fifty years later, to find a rhyme for "entertainer" in "legendary, lovely Marlene."

One of the earliest published family pictures of Dietrich, about two or three years old, shows her in a lace dress, with an inordinately long waist-sash, her hair pulled firmly back by ribbons to reveal a quite surprisingly determined face. Her ankle socks are wrinkled, an engaging imperfection reinforced by the pose, for she is leaning back, in an attitude that was to be refined much later into her world-weary trademark, against what looks like the end of a child's brass bedstead, grasping the two uprights very firmly indeed.

Frau Dietrich dominated the comfortable household in Berlin's upper-middle-class Schöneberg district. She had been seventeen at the time of her marriage in 1883, and even sixty-two years later she was to be described by the U.S. Army officer who located her living not far from a bomb- and canon-blitzed Berlin as "a tiny woman, but with great animation, fire, and drive." She was well read—particularly strong on the German Romantics—and had a talent for running her household, which included a visiting governess for the two girls until they were old enough for school. (Elisabeth, Marlene's elder sister, later became a teacher, and the only sign of *her* celebrity status was that she was held under house arrest at Belsen, though not actually in the infamous camp itself, as part of Hitler's vaguely formulated scheme for holding the kith and kin of celebrated Germans as handy hostages.)

"Discipline" and "duty" were what home life was all about. Dietrich later claimed that her mother had made acting difficult for her, since her upbringing put such emphasis on *suppressing* her feelings, in the polite bourgeois tradition, rather than exposing them. What her mother did, in fact, was to "set" Marlene's acting style very early on in life; it was the very concealment of her feelings that helped her project a marvelously potent allure of distant mystery. The last slap on the face she received from her mother in the way of discipline arose from this need to mask her feelings, she told the English journalist Charles Graves in 1936.[1] "I was having dancing lessons and had to dance with everyone in the room, including a young man whom I did not like, nor his dancing either. I made a long face. Mother saw it and slapped me as soon as we were alone. 'You must not show your feelings, it is bad manners,' she said." Obedience was the overriding rule in the Dietrich home: pleasures had to be earned before they could be enjoyed. She was not entirely unprepared when, years later, she met her mentor in a film director who also enforced strict obedience and demanded that she love a man without letting her sentiments show.

There were smaller but more practical bonuses from this home training: when asked, in 1936, what conditions had been like while filming *The Garden of Allah* in the burning desert around Yuma, Arizona, she replied, "I was never thirsty. I was trained not to be . . . ever since I was a small girl. I was never allowed to complain." The film's director, Richard Boleslawski, unaccustomed to such ingrained fortitude, drank some of the desert water, caught an infection and died soon after finishing the film.

Part of Dietrich's childhood was spent in Weimar, a capital of humanism and culture—Goethe and Liszt had lived there—about 150 miles from Berlin. Why the family moved to Weimar, or how long they spent there, is not clear: it sounds like a temporary posting, part of Lieutenant Dietrich's anticipated police promotion, for Marlene was soon back in Berlin as a day pupil at the Viktoria-Luise School for Girls, where she was drilled in Goethe's blend of high ideals and hard work and temporarily infected by one female teacher's infatuation for the Italian actress Eleonora Duse.

In a rare outburst of recall, contained in an article which she wrote for a West German newspaper nearly seventy years later, Dietrich complained that her schoolmates had made her feel unsure of herself. She was one of 300 pupils, some of them from well-to-do families, who were collected in private carriages. Perhaps to ease her sense of (comparative) social disadvantage, she began making herself look older than she was. Not so many years later, Greta Gustafsson—not yet renamed Garbo—also set out to compensate for the feelings of inferiority bred by her slum background by catching the eye of her peers in flamboyant clothes that made her look older. Ironic to think how both stars would do exactly the opposite when their careers got under way!

The premature death of Lieutenant Dietrich in 1911—cause unknown—did nothing to help Marlene's adolescent insecurity. But Frau Dietrich seems to have been inordinately attracted to men in uniform: she remarried with some rapidity, this time Eduard von Losch, a colonel in the Grenadiers. There are also several minor mysteries connected with this marriage. Though the Felsings were well-to-do, and Frau Dietrich's original dowry (for which every German girl in pre-World War I days was supposed to keep herself chaste as virginal collateral) had been generous, she appears at this time to have been short of money. Perhaps it had all been spent on supplementing a higher life-style than her first husband's policeman's pay could sustain. She had therefore taken employment as housekeeper to the Von Losch family; and it was there that she met her second husband. It may be that the Von Losch family were distant relatives of the Felsings.

The outbreak of the 1914 war made for a predominantly matriarchal household dominated by thoughts of "the men at the front." Marlene spent hours knitting warm garments for the German troops or accompanying her school choir to the railroad station to sing the boys off to battle with a patriotic anthem. But it was the aura of war, rather than loyalty to any particular side fighting in it, which commanded her sentimental allegiances. One day, on a country excursion with her classmates, she spotted French prisoners of war confined behind barbed wire. The young girl plucked some white wild roses and pressed them into the prisoners' hands as they stretched them through the wire to accept what were to them, no doubt, mementos of their own absent children's innocence.

In 1915, Marlene was confirmed in the Lutheran faith. By now she was playing the violin and displaying a talent that made her mother consider a career for her as a professional musician. Violin playing is an art that requires arduous repetitions of the same bars of music. It was to be good training for the way she was later made to utter a single line of dialogue, or maybe even a single word like "Yes," in front of the camera dozens of times until her exacting director decided the resonance was right.

A more ambiguous instance of where her tastes were taking her is contained in a photograph dating from 1917, when she was sixteen and the leader of the school orchestra. The students had staged a tableau of Spanish musicians, playing the tune "La Paloma," which the Emperor Maximilian of Mexico had requested just before his execution fifty years earlier. Accompanied by a tambourine quartet, Dietrich played the melody on her violin while dressed in a male costume consisting of sombrero, embroidered jacket, and knee breeches. The costume was not as audacious as the trouser suits that were to hang in her closet in the years ahead, but it was an interesting hint of the public *travestie* she would later display with such studied unconcern on the screen and in the street at a time when women wearing men's clothes in public brought a stiff warning from no less a figure than the Prefect of Paris.

When she graduated from school in 1918, her mother enrolled her at the Berlin Hochschule für Musik. She stayed only a few months. The panic and despair spreading through Berlin as the Imperial German army's resistance collapsed induced anyone with no pressing business—and violin playing was hardly that—to flee the city for safety. (This probably explains why the Hochschule für Musik has no record of Dietrich's enrollment.) Her mother moved rapidly to evacuate herself and the children to the relative safety of Weimar, which she knew from her first husband's spell of duty there. Soon came another calamity: Frau von Losch was widowed a second time.

Like nearly every major event affecting Dietrich for some years to come, there are at least two versions of her stepfather's death; and the confusion testifies to how virtues that were far from bourgeois came to be injected into her life history by error, or possibly intention, so that Dietrich's social origins eventually were made to seem more adventurous, even illustrious, than those to which a later and plainer generation of film stars could (or would) lay claim. In some reports, Colonel von Losch is "amalgamated" with Dietrich's natural father. In others, he dies in battle on the Russian front; in others still, he is repatriated in a badly wounded condition and later retires. The most colorful account is one attributed to the film star herself, in 1937, in which "Captain Dietrich" (*sic*) is first wounded in France, convalesces at the Schloss of his "friend" the Duke of Brunswick, and later, after being twice wounded on the Eastern Front, gets blood poisoning from a rusty telephone wire that had been applied as a makeshift tourniquet. According to this story, Marlene's mother, who has set out for the battlefront, arrives in the middle of a Russian advance, meets the medical staff in full flight, but presses gallantly ahead and finds her husband lying in the hay of a cottage barn. He dies, is buried at Kovno on the Russian front, but his remains are later exhumed and reinterred in a private graveyard at Dessau, in Anhalt, where the father-in-law of Dietrich's mother had served as court chamberlain to the Duke of Anhalt. Dietrich does not seem to have repeated this rather romantic account ever again.

13

The school violinist garbed à *l'espagnole*, 1917. In the graduation photograph of 1918, Dietrich is the second from right in the front row.

What *can* be said with certainty is that Von Losch did not live to see the social changes that profoundly altered his country and his family's way of life in the aftermath of war; and for all the memories Dietrich has provided about their effects on her, she might have been living in another country. Nothing has come from her about her parent's privations, save a reference to the enforced frugality of boiled potatoes as the basis of every meal; nothing about her own state of mind at her family's sudden pitch into social (and soon economic) chaos. Her tongue relaxed in later years just sufficiently to explain why her musical ambitions were abruptly dashed: but even this explanation has varied, one version attributing her abandonment of the violin to a ganglion (or knot) developing on her wrist, another to her pulling a ligament between her fingers, and yet a third to some chastening criticism of her playing which she received. Whatever the truth, she was back in Berlin by 1920.

What her character and temperament were like now becomes a matter of even more contradictory witness. The documentary evidence that has survived the 1914–18 war is extremely tenuous. There is her graduation photograph of 1918, a group picture showing Dietrich as an oval-faced girl, plumpish in the commonplace way of those pre-diet-conscious days, but again markedly strong-featured with her prominent eyebrows already defined and her hair rolled upwards to expose a strong width of brow. Her face in this informal photograph is entirely devoid of animated expression. Some of the girls wear the faint smiles of the self-conscious on such occasions, or look to right or left with alert expressions that are independent of the photographer's no doubt harassing instructions. Dietrich, almost alone in the group, appears intensely self-absorbed.

Unlike Greta Garbo, who had gone to work in a backstreet barber's shop in Stockholm when barely out of her childhood years, Dietrich was sheltered from much direct experience of the world until the postwar crises of the Weimar Republic. Middle-class convention and a stable society had stressed the chastity that a girl from a good family must at all costs preserve (or be believed to preserve) until marriage. Accordingly, no boyfriends enter the picture in her later schooldays: in any case, all eligible young men were rushed off to serve on the war front. They would not come back, except as casualties or permanent invalids, until the great trek home of more than two million footsore, beaten and sullen soldiers who created the post-Armistice legions of the unemployed.

Marlene has confessed to having entertained a few romantic crushes, but they were on members of her own sex. In one of the rare articles published under her own name (in a Königsberg newspaper in 1931, after she had become an international star), she remembered her schoolgirlish fascination with the actress Henny Porten, Germany's prewar "Mary Pickford," whose innocence triumphed over worldly hardships and ultimately brought her the rewards of happiness and marriage. Marlene used to paint picture postcards of the actress.

She also wrote fan letters to her. On one occasion she was even said to have serenaded her idol on the violin, standing under a window in the snow of wintry

Garmisch, where the star was in residence for the skiing. But apparently the melodious but importunate fan had pushed her luck too far: one glance out of the window, and the shutters were abruptly closed. Some time later, when Dietrich had become a name in films, she met Henny Porten and felt once more that intensified sense of existing—"like being in an elevator and going down very fast."

For the moment, though, she needed all the perseverance that had been drilled into her simply to get through each day. Berlin was a particularly bad place to be in 1919–20. Its population was ravaged by bitter cold and the hunger caused by the continuing Allied blockade—nearly 700,000 people died in Germany of malnutrition within six months of the Armistice. As part of the raging influenza pandemic, 2,000 people died in a single day. There were a quarter-million unemployed men in the capital, discontented recruits for the recurring *putsches* like the Spartakus uprising against the Republican Government in 1919 or the Kapp attempt at a takeover the following year. A single rumor could start a panic; for the Allies were threatening occupation if the terms of the Versailles Peace Settlement, humiliating for Germany, were not agreed to forthwith. Hoarders and black marketeers speculated amidst the uncertainties, and this plunder ate into the middle classes' last reserves of capital and dignity. "The German people," wrote Count Kessler, "were reeling deliriously between blank despair, frenzied rivalry and revolution. Berlin had become a nightmare, a carnival of jazz bands and rattling machine guns. . . . Profiteers and their girls, the scum and riffraff of half Europe . . . could be seen growing fat and sleek and flaunting their new cars and ostentatious jewelry in the faces of the pale children and starving women shivering in their rags before empty bakers' and butchers' shops."

Worse was to come. Inflation soared in the middle of 1921. From under 400 marks to the dollar, the exchange rate escalated in a delirium of dizzy zeroes to over 1.3 trillion marks two years later and then up, up, up to over four trillion before stabilization was achieved at the end of 1923 simply by striking out the dozen noughts on every bill and pegging the rate at the prewar level. By then, German society had been transformed by fear and despair. Loss of faith in one's money was the material corollary of a loss of faith in one's way of life. Old values became as "worthless" as the old currency. The earliest, and most enduring, effect of this was to free women from the constraints that had equated sexual chastity with economic value. When money was valueless, virginity had no premium put on it; if a girl's family could not get together a stable dowry, the whole marriage system collapsed. Many a respectable bourgeois daughter, who had already been compelled to support her family by doing jobs she had considered socially demeaning before the war, quickly learned to make use of her talent, or simply her sex, in professions that were once considered to be beyond mention. Prostitution boomed. The numbers of amateurs plying their trade on the thoroughfares of Berlin—the "Babylon of the world," as Stefan Zweig called it at the time—provided the visible sensation of vice for those who did not wish to partake of its satisfactions. "Novelty" was sometimes a more accurate way of characterizing the thrusting new life-styles than "immorality." But when novelty itself was in tumultuous supply, the sheer energy it released swept away conventions. "The German people were living as if at a railroad station," said the Russian refugee poet Ilya Ehrenburg, "no one knowing what would happen the next day."

Yet of all this tumult, its fears, degradations, insecurities and opportunities, Marlene Dietrich has spoken scarcely a word. It's as if she had suffered some attack of temporary amnesia. In this era, though, the "other Dietrich" was almost certainly formed. The postwar revolution that changed the face of Berlin society changed the nature of the girl who had been so carefully nurtured in the bosom of bourgeois certainties. By blocking conventional outlets for a girl of her class and attainments, the chaos liberated other undefined aspects of young Marlene and articulated them into the development of a personality that became far more bohemian than bourgeois. Perseverance was modulated into opportunism; a training in classical music was transposed into the impromptu tempo of cabaret shows conceived to mock the notion of a problematical tomorrow; and in that traditionally cynical capital city, which adjusted its expectations of life to the short-term lessons of experience, Dietrich learned to rely on other attributes than the ones which the daughter and stepdaughter respectively of Prussian army officers might have used to make her way in society.

The testimony of a few surviving friends of that era suggests that she moved out of the family home, shared a rented room and lived on the largely carbohydrate diet of times of scarcity. She kept out the cold with a mass of conglomerate garments and picked up casual jobs paying small wages. In addition, she put her musicianship to use, playing the violin in theater orchestras or providing mood music for the silent films that were now pouring out of giant production companies like UFA.

It is more than likely that Dietrich simply drifted into stage and screen work from these hand-to-mouth beginnings. It rings truer than the usually accepted tale of an aristocratic family suddenly confronted by a daughter determined to sacrifice birth and upbringing to the raffish public display of her untested theatrical talents. After all, it is no great step from the orchestra pit at a stage revue to a place in the chorus line, especially if the legs are as young and pretty as those Dietrich kicked up. As soon as the strange theater world becomes familiar territory, a new sense of personal identity is engendered. And when one's education is as well grounded as Dietrich's, one naturally seeks to progress, not necessarily from the chorus line to the leading role, but from the musical stage to the serious theater.

It is known that Dietrich danced in the touring companies of Guido Thielscher, who provided the larger provincial German cities with the illusion of metropolitan titillation—this was probably in the winter of 1921. Then, emboldened by her grounding in German and foreign literature—she could already speak good French and reasonable English—and perhaps lured on by the

Berlin's theater life in the 1920s was dominated by Max Reinhardt (*left*), who put on lavish spectacles in the Grosses Schauspielhaus (*above, left*). Dietrich studied with one of Reinhardt's assistant directors and was soon playing in minor roles in Reinhardt productions.

Germany's runaway inflation provided the Hungarian artist László Moholy-Nagy with the motif for a collage of nearly worthless banknotes.

intoxication of self-display that even cheaply mounted musicals induce, she applied for admission to Max Reinhardt's drama school in Berlin's Schumannstrasse. Reinhardt, then forty-eight, was an impresario in the empire-building mold. He directed the fortunes of several theaters: the Deutsches Theater; the Kammerspiele, next door, for experimental drama; and a former circus arena, the Grosses Schauspielhaus, seating up to 3,000, and allowing full rein to his penchant for putting on spectacles rather than plays of ideas and moral thrust. Reinhardt was an institution as well as an individual, able to "franchise" his "method," which was to set players resonating with the appropriate emotions and then fine-tune them into the most telling combination of sentiments. His school taught diction, elocution and rhythmic dancing—things familiar to any girl who had a "good" schooling such as Dietrich's. Her initial approach was appropriately high-toned: she read an excerpt from Hugo von Hofmannsthal's *Der Tor und der Tod* (*Death and the Fool*), then recited Gretchen's prayer to the Virgin from Goethe's *Faust*. But Reinhardt apparently did not feel she was ready yet, though he made no objection when one of his assistant directors offered to take Marlene for private lessons. This apprenticeship enabled her to apply for stage and film work, using the Reinhardt connection.

Dietrich had already developed ways of drawing attention to herself. Shy girls often do, when necessity compels them to make the effort. About this time, too, Greta Garbo was singling herself out from her classmates at the Swedish Royal Dramatic Academy—in contrast to Dietrich, she was accepted at first try by the theater establishment—by virtue of wearing *outré* clothes and striking other attention-getting postures. Dietrich would join the other girls in the waiting lines of casting offices clad in an extra-long boa, or a hat with a preposterous feather, or simply leading a small, yappish dog on a leash—anything to catch a casting director's eye. She seems to have been what the French usefully describe as *journalière*: one day attractively dressed in smart street clothes, the next rather bohemian in her makeup and costume. She changed moods as often as wardrobes. If friends are to be believed, there was a troubled nature behind this erratic presentation of herself; she was said to veer from depression to elation, sometimes comporting herself with punk-like vivacity, at other moments seemingly feeling the constraints of her bourgeois upbringing. Perhaps her mother's influence on her waxed and waned this way, too. She was learning the tricks of making herself sexually attractive. Contemporaries recall that she could be quite flirtatious.

When did Dietrich have her first professional encounter with a movie camera? If we are to believe an account, extraordinary in its sense of vivid recall, which was first published in an English newspaper in 1935, she made an impromptu screen test in the summer of 1922. It was conducted by a young photographer, Stefan Lorant, who had entered the German film industry after the war and who would later become a power in the field of picture magazines when he reached England in the early 1930s and guided Sir Edward Hulton's pioneering magazine *Picture Post* to its preeminent position in photojournalism. Lorant recalled receiving a phone call from an unnamed film director friend of his about "a nice young girl . . . I want you to be kind to her. I know her family very well. She wants to become a film actress and I want you to make a test of her."[2]

Lorant was then shooting a silent film in the "glasshouse" sheds designed to admit every gleam of sunlight at Berlin's Tempelhof Field studios. Emerging into the refreshing air from the sauna-like conditions on the interior set, he discovered a young girl who had been waiting for him, looking "lively as quicksilver, a very whirlwind of vivacity." Dietrich was then twenty-one and her determination was impressive. She had come for her test, she said, and she intended to get it. According to Lorant, she clung to his side and badgered him as the tired man tried to pack up his equipment and leave for home. "I've been so looking forward to this day," she said, with tears in her eyes. "I didn't sleep all night—and now you're sending me away." She said she wanted to go into films "because I feel that's what I was born to do." Lorant tried dissuasion: the exhausting work, the heat, the uphill grind before one's name appears on the posters, the feeling that one is an object and hardly a human being. "I'm not going to let that discourage me," the girl answered in a confident voice. "Please, please, Mr. Lorant, make a test of me."

Unwilling to return to the inferno of the film set, Lorant set his camera up outdoors and ordered the girl to climb on to a nearby fence and then, when ordered, to jump down again. "What for?" she asked in astonishment. "Don't ask silly questions. Do you want to be a film actress or not?" "Yes." "Then do as I tell you." (Already she was hearing the note of command that would later be used on her like a trainer's whip.) There then ensued a sad, semisadistic game in which the girl was made to perform for Lorant's camera while the professional actors who had just come off work and were still suffering from the heat stood round and stared and felt their frayed nerves soothed by the pains that were being heaped on this neophyte. Lorant wrote:

Marlene must have been made to get up on the fence some fifteen times, and jump down again, and while doing this, she had to laugh, cry, grimace, scream, sob. But [she] didn't mind at all. She jumped down from the fence, she jumped into the ditch, she hopped and skipped and shouted for joy. It all seemed great fun to us at the time. We were revenging ourselves on this innocent victim for the sufferings we had endured. We did not feel so tired any more. . . . After we had made her jump enough, I took a really serious shot of her, a close-up of her head. There was something menacing about the broad, high, Slavonic cheekbones. . . . [She] turned her head from right to left, like a mannequin at a fashion parade. When her eyes met the lens of the camera, she had to laugh. She screwed up her mouth, then she turned her head further round into profile. "That'll do, my child, the test is over."

Lorant dismissed her, telling her the result of the test would be known at the end of the week. When he screened it privately for himself and some friends,

we had a good laugh at the funny way the young thing jumped up and down from the fence. In the close-up, the girl who was quite pretty in real life looked distinctly ugly. Broad face, expressionless eyes, uncouth movements. The opinion was unanimous. No

A studio portrait, c. 1923, undoubtedly made for the eyes of casting directors. "She was learning the tricks of making herself sexually attractive."

20

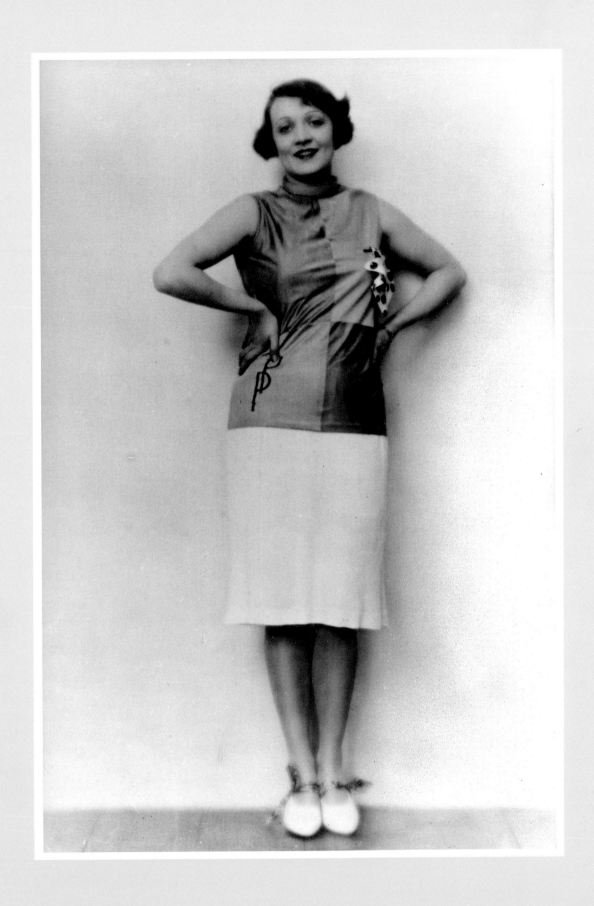

talent whatsoever. . . . The director who had recommended her notified her, as painlessly as possible, that she was quite unsuitable. She disappeared. If I had given her a thought at all, I should only have imagined her married to some shop assistant or bank clerk in the provinces . . .

This is a remarkable recollection: a very detailed and convincing testimony to Dietrich's desire to succeed and the pains and humiliations she was prepared to accept in achieving her aim. Later accounts of her alleged indifference to stardom have to be seen in the context of this early one. Having been hurt once when relatively defenseless, she now wore "indifference" like defensive armor plating. The lesson, "Don't show your feelings," contributed to her businesslike approach and, ultimately, to her art and image. A year or so later, Lorant ran across her in the street: now he saw a girl who was more serious, less spirited and vivacious (and probably far less innocent). "She told me she had actually managed to 'get on the films' and that she was having a hard struggle. 'Why don't you do something else?' 'No,' and her eyes flashed. 'I'll get there yet.'"

This second encounter was probably in 1923. She had already played minor roles in two Reinhardt company productions, *The Taming of the Shrew* and *A Midsummer Night's Dream*; but her first film was in *Der kleine Napoleon* (*The Little Napoleon*: 1923), as the maid who helps her mistress (played by one Antonia Dietrich, but no relation) to escape the lecherous clutches of Napoleon's younger brother Jerome. "Nonhistorical comedies," flirting with famous figures of history and sumptuously costumed, were in vogue. Foreign audiences liked them; and the hard currency they earned did more for the balance sheets of UFA than did domestic revenues so eroded by inflation that they totaled a mere ten percent of production costs. UFA had strong official incentives to export its own productions; and as the country could not afford to import foreign films, the German cinema was enjoying boom conditions. Dietrich thus entered German films at a time of abundant production and was to quit them at just the moment when Hollywood's resurgence as a power in the new era of the talkies enabled it to impose its monopolistic vigor on even the overseas markets it thought it had lost with the coming of sound. Her next film showed how luck favored her in other ways as well.

Tragödie der Liebe (*Tragedy of Love*: 1923) was directed by Joe May, whose wife Mia was an established star—an asset that permitted his film company to enjoy more than usually lavish backing from the major distributors of its films. It employed a permanent staff, among them a general factotum (officially listed as "assistant director") named Rudolf Sieber. A young Czech *bon vivant* and ladies' man, much cultivated by aspiring actresses for the say-so he possessed (or laid claim to) over bit parts in the movies, Sieber was supervising an audition when a girl appeared, tugging a reluctant pet dog and wearing furs in a style designed more to express personality than keep the wearer warm. They were "show" clothes worn, like the currently fashionable monocles that some girls sported, to catch the eye. They caught Sieber's eye.

Tragödie der Liebe was over 200 minutes long, shot in four parts and released in two sections in March and May 1923. It starred Emil Jannings, then at the start of his film career, using his already burly (and soon gross) body to brilliant physical effect as a maniacally jealous professional wrestler who hurls his mistress's lover from a rooftop in Paris and is arraigned and condemned at a sensational trial attended by "le tout Paris." Dietrich played the mistress of the presiding judge. It was little more than a spectator role, literally and figuratively, but the kind whose importance grows with what the player makes of it.

By all accounts, Dietrich used her wits (and maybe Sieber's professional advice) to advance herself from sidelines to close-up. She establishes herself right away as a skittish creature, but able to bend men the way she wills, by telling her lover the judge to get her a front-row seat at the trial. She wears a monocle and a feather boa of the flamboyant sort that girls were wont to flaunt as emblems of their "liberated" status in Kurfürstendamm café society. At the trial itself, she is in the gallery and engaged in by-play that compels the camera to single her out from the sea of faces for its special attention. Her monocle is supplemented by opera glasses, the better to see Jannings: thus her inconsequential part is tied directly in interest to the film's "money" star. The judge's composure is disturbed by seeing his mistress flirtatiously encouraging the fancy of a new man in her vicinity—a piece of brazen frivolity judged "very Berlin" in its unconcealed cynicism.

This comic cameo offered relief from Jannings's weightier dramatics. And it did so in a film which Peter Panter, in the influential *Die Weltbühne*, called "the best and most realistic German detective film yet made."[3] Paul Leni's production design was impressive; and Jannings drew especial praise for the "homely little gestures" he used to humanize his role and for the hint of self-abasement (which he was later to make into his cinematic *forte*) when he sinks to his knees and embraces the laddered-stockinged legs of a chambermaid who is swathing herself sensuously in his present of a fur coat. Six years later, Jannings would be in much the same posture of erotic abasement before Dietrich; she, however, would receive his affections much more imperiously and repay them far more cruelly. "A great achievement of Emil's," wrote one of Germany's best critics, Kurt Tucholsky.[4]

Dietrich herself was not yet garnering praise in print: but no matter, her "possibilities" were visible. She was on her way. With this film as her "calling card," her career now really took off. She was admitted into Reinhardt's company and appeared (as Mrs. Shenstone) in Maugham's play *The Circle* at the impresario's Kammerspiele experimental theater, whose intimacy must have had a bearing on the refinement of her acting style. "If an actor needs to lift his whole arm at the Großes Schauspielhaus," wrote the critic Heinz Herald, "he need only move his hand at the Deutsches Theater; and at the Kammerspiele, it's enough if he moves a finger."[5]

The next film she appeared in was an updated version of the Good Samaritan parable, *Der Mensch am Wege* (*The Man at the Roadside*: 1923), directed by Wilhelm

(Hollywood's future "William") Dieterle. In this she wore her blonde hair in tight braids, an unbecoming style she adopted in later starring roles when she was required to look like a young *ingénue* or else (as here) a peasant girl. Set against the world-weary sophistication that was to become her trademark, such utility makeup always looked implausible—but less so, perhaps, in this early incarnation.

Her career could have gone either way—stage or films—in the middle of 1923, for she suddenly got a run of good theater roles in plays by Bjørnson (*When the New Vines Flower*), Molière (*Le Malade imaginaire*) and, in 1924, Wedekind (*Spring Awakening*), playing respectively a girl whose sexuality starts rising like the sap in the vineyard; a pert and seductively fidgety maid; and an artist's model and amateur prostitute. In this last part, critics praised her starkly realistic portrayal of sex for sale, evocative of the real thing on the thoroughfares just outside the theater. Another role was one she had prepared herself for: marriage to Rudolf Sieber.

It was preceded by the film *Der Sprung ins Leben* (*Leap into Life*: 1924), in which Dietrich plays a lovelorn girl whose heart beats in time to a risk-taking circus acrobat. Its chief importance was to provide the cash for her wedding in that terrifying year of inflation. She and Sieber were married, at a Lutheran service, on May 17, 1924, held in the Kaiser Wilhelm Gedächtniskirche. (Sieber was Roman Catholic; his church did not permit the marriage of any member to an unconverted man or woman of a different faith.) It appears to have been a hastily arranged event: reports have it that the guests arrived late and that Dietrich's wedding dress did not fit her well. The couple moved into an apartment block at 54 Kaiserallee, not far from Dietrich's old home. A neighbor was Leni Riefenstahl, future cinematic chronicler of National Socialist Germany. What Dietrich's family thought of the match is unknown: but sheer survival came before social connections in those lean times. Sieber had good professional contacts and, with currency reform taking successful effect the same year, it turned out to be a good time to get married.

If Dietrich had nourished any thought of retiring into domesticity—and her mother's strongly conventional attitudes seem to have still been influential—her resolution did not last. She paused only long enough to have a baby, a daughter named Heidede, born in January 1925, then stepped into a small role, little more than a walk-on part and further diminished in the editing, in *Die freudlose Gasse* (*Joyless Street*: 1925), which G. W. Pabst was shooting in Berlin that winter. It was to be Greta Garbo's *envoi* to European filmmaking before she sailed for America the same summer.

Dietrich's momentum continued. Though eleventh in the cast list of her next film, Arthur Robson's *Manon Lescaut* (1926), her role as the nobleman's mistress was actually the second female lead. This was another sumptuous production (decor again by Paul Leni), a crowd pleaser which succeeded through Lubitsch-style comedy in making its impact at the box office despite its loose grip on history

A trio of early films. The tousled girl holding the hand phone is twenty-two-year-old Marlene Dietrich in *Tragödie der Liebe*. In *Der Mensch am Wege* (below) she was cast as a young peasant girl, seen here with Wilhelm Dieterle, who both directed and played a leading role. The film that followed, *Der Sprung ins Leben* (above, left), had only a tiny part for the fledgling actress, but it provided the wherewithal for her wedding to Rudolf Sieber.

(there are, for instance, patriotic Parisians chorusing the "Marseillaise" two generations before it was written). Dietrich had a more active role in it than the passive Lya de Putti, who played what one German critic called the "sweet doll's figure" of Manon. Dietrich's manner of playing was helping to establish her style in German films; but it was a very different style from the one by which the world later knew her. In those days she was all high-spirited, sexy coquettishness; she dressed in low-cut and off-the-shoulder gowns; she taunted her female rival in love; she made seductive eyes at men in cafés and casinos. She was also catching the critics' eyes. "The exceptionally pretty [*ungewöhnlich hübsche*] Marlene Dietrich," Roland Schacht noted in the *Berliner Zeitung*, adding, "one would like to see [her] again very soon."[6] *Manon Lescaut* became the first film of Dietrich's to be shown in America, at the end of 1926, largely of course on Lya de Putti's reputation in that country as the star of Griffith's *Sorrows of Satan* in 1926.

Yet another coquette role followed, consolidating her reputation but with the inevitable typecasting implications. The difference in *Eine Du Barry von Heute* (*A Modern Du Barry*: 1926) was that this time she played her role in contemporary not historical finery: ermine wraps and evening gowns covered with sequins. She looked like a Kurfürstendamm Clara Bow as she jiggled her body to the Jazz Age rhythms of the "black music," and of Miss Josephine Baker in particular, which were galvanizing Berlin night life at the time and which accompanied this silent film in the larger cinemas. But the tale of a king falling for a flirt of a flowergirl was variable. Its director, Alexander Korda, intended it as a vehicle for his wife Maria, but he and his scenarist, Lajos Biro, could not sustain the modern (and Berlin-like) note of cynicism directed at an opportunistic society where the right dress allows the borrower to hold court in the best circles. "Up to the middle it's a film for today," wrote Hans Feld in the *Berliner Börsen-Courier*, "and at the end it's a Du Barry of yesterday."[7] Dietrich, as the cocotte whose *haute couture* gown is appropriated by Maria Korda, was billed, either by accident or (unrepeated) experiment, as "Marlaine."

Her part in *A Modern Du Barry* is not large, and very likely got smaller during or after the shooting, since Korda would have been reluctant to take any attention away from his wife. But Dietrich, toting her *lorgnette* again, plays "spoilt" with amusing flair, and shows a heart beneath all the worldly wisdom by counseling the *ingénue* not to discard the old lover until the new suitor is thoroughly fascinated. There is one visually memorable moment: about to enter a sumptuous drawing room through floor-to-ceiling French windows, Dietrich pauses to scrutinize the room and the people in it, and for a few seconds leans slackly yet provocatively against the window in a posture as characteristic of the later star as a signature in an autograph book.

The year 1926 kept her exceptionally busy. She played another Berlin flapper in Korda's *Madame wünscht keine Kinder* (*Madame Doesn't Want Children*: 1926), though it was only as a "dress extra" for a party scene and probably undertaken out of gratitude for Korda's engaging Rudi Sieber as his production assistant.

26

Dietrich's first film to reach America was *Manon Lescaut*, but her role as the coquettish Micheline (*left*) was distinctly secondary to that of the star Lya de Putti. In *Eine du Barry von Heute* (*below*) she "looked like a Kurfürstendamm Clara Bow."

Then she made her first significant stage appearance in a show that continued to set her typical style. Stepping into a pair of high-heeled sequined shoes and dressed in the height of contemporary camp, she played the mistress of ceremonies in a titillating extravaganza, *Von Mund zu Mund* (*From Mouth to Mouth*), written by Erik Charell (of *White Horse Inn* fame). It ran for four hours and contained nearly twenty scenes of teasing content. One of her co-stars was a muscular *chanteuse* and "drag queen" named Claire Waldoff. Just as Garbo modeled *her* low and mournful register in talking pictures on the style of the Swedish actress Naima Wifstrand, so Dietrich is reputed to have adopted her own lower, indeed almost gruff, singing register from the challenging manner of Fräulein Waldoff. Perhaps, too, this is one of the sources of her insouciant stage *hauteur*, daring anyone to drop their attention for a moment. As Waldoff did, Dietrich later insisted on table service being suspended while she was enrapturing the clientele in restaurants and nightclubs with her act. She learned quickly, and early, how to impose herself, as well as pose.

After the show, Dietrich would often go out on the town, accompanied by her compliant husband and friends, seeking the fashionable entertainment of transvestite clubs, where women performing in men's clothes attracted even larger audiences than did women performing in no clothes at all. This kind of entertainment was characteristic of the double standards of morality as well as gender. One needed little knowledge of a foreign language to appreciate its lubricious artfulness, and swarms of tourists helped fuel the city's nightclub boom. A favorite place for Dietrich and her party to unwind after their own extravagant but slightly more orthodox show was the Eldorado Club, somewhat inappropriately located on Martin Lutherstrasse. There, every one of the hat-check girls, waitresses and barmaids was a female impersonator or a transsexual. "Any Berlin lady of the evening might turn out to be a man," Anita Loos recorded, while Stefan Zweig noted that along the Kurfürstendamm "young men, powdered and rouged, sauntered . . . not all professionals. Every schoolboy wanted to earn some money."

The delirium accompanying the "economic apocalypse" of a few years earlier had now been institutionalized as a self-perpetuating sex-service industry selling all manner of perverse thrills. Dubious "sexologists" like Dr. Magnus Hirschfeld, who operated from a pseudo-scientific Academy for Sexual Research strategically sited on the edge of the Tiergarten, turned a magnifying and distorting mirror back on to the capital's aberrant aspects by publicizing (and inevitably popularizing) sexual deviancy. He gave special attention to female homosexuality. Dietrich's later, publicly indulged penchant for wearing male attire was no sudden aberration; indeed, she didn't see it as an aberration at all, habitually declaring that men's wear was simply more comfortable and cheaper than the clothes women bought. It can also be viewed as simply the prevailing "orthodoxy" that Berliners expected of those who entertained them in the permissive 1920s.

The Kurfürstendamm at night—Berlin's Great White Way in its Weimar Republic heyday. In the foreground is the Gloria Palast, a huge movie theater built to resemble a German castle, where *Der blaue Engel* had its première in April 1930.

Meantime, she rushed through two films shot "back to back" by a woman producer, Ellen Richter, famed for her flapper-type plots filled with "wild parties," *déclassé* nobility and a hectic atmosphere of infidelity. These were very popular in Central Europe and a staple of UFA's production roster. Dietrich played a French flirt in *Kopf hoch, Charly!* (*Head Up, Charly!*: 1927), but a more substantial role in *Der Juxbaron* (*The Bogus Baron*: 1927). Its hero was the popular star Reinhold Schünzel, cast as an impostor who passes himself off as a gentleman by wearing the right clothes and adopting the right manners. (It was the favorite plot of Central European farceurs and comic-opera librettists and was to enjoy a long run in its Americanized versions, such as Joan Crawford's 1937 comedy *The Bride Wore Red*, so long as Hollywood's first-generation moguls of European extraction reigned in their studios.) Dietrich played the second lead as the family's eligible daughter who imagines she is making a rich and noble match. Sporting a monocle once again, she took to farce with surprisingly self-parodying brio, and the film, a lively comedy that looked costly, was widely shown. Being associated with a hit like this didn't harm her—though an accumulation of such roles would be responsible for some of the reservations shown in casting the German film that would eventually shape her destiny.

Meanwhile, she was very much a part of the prevailing fashion in Berlin show business, which was now being dominated by the novel sensations imported from America, or more correctly Broadway. That very name, suggesting bright lights, smart life and syncopated rhythms, not to mention sex, violence and hedonism that didn't count the consequences, was the show-business collateral of the very rapid investment which American companies had made in the German economy. The Dawes Plan had opened up the country to international financiers in 1924. The rhythms of American big business were to be heard orchestrating the theater scene, too, and the 1927 production of *Broadway*, a George Abbott and Philip Dunning musical play about gangsters, chorus girls, bootleggers and jazz musicians, added a note that was exotic yet familiar—Times Square had come to the Ku'damm.

Dietrich played one of the chorines of Nick Vedris's Paradise Club. She prepared herself for the role with a thoroughness that was to be typical of her whole career. She took tap-dancing lessons as if she were being drilled on a Prussian barracks square, sweated it out in a men's gymnasium and created a sensation in the musical when she lay supine on the stage and pedaled her legs very rapidly in the air in what was meant to be a limbering-up exercise but had other associations for some of those who were mesmerized by the spotlit provocativeness of her limbs. Dietrich was one of those players who seem to know intuitively how to take the scene away from others in the show simply by a look or a prop or a piece of perfect timing. Some of her later directors were to refine this talent: but it was there from the start.

By now her name was well known to impresarios; her face and figure were greeted with impatient appreciation by the Berlin public. All this was possible, of

Dietrich played a monocled French flirt in *Kopf hoch, Charly!* (*above*, with Angelo Ferrari, Toni Tetzlaff, and—swathed in white fur—the film's leading lady and producer, Ellen Richter). In her next film, *Der Juxbaron*, she had a more important though still secondary role as an "eligible daughter who imagines she is making a rich and noble match" (*middle* and *below*, with Reinhold Schünzel as the bogus baron). Dietrich was in the process of becoming type-cast as a pert flapper.

course, only because her husband was acquiescent and content to help run the home and look after their child while his wife ran her career, reverting with periodic and frenzied energy to being a *Hausfrau* and putting in several days' cooking, cleaning and mothering of little Heidede. When *Broadway* went on tour and opened in Vienna in mid-1927, Dietrich took over the important role of Pearl, the chorine who shoots her lover's killer with the bitter command, "Turn round, rat. I don't want to give it to you like you gave it to him—in the back." A woman killing for love, revenging herself for her man, and doing it all according to the code of criminal honor: it is the earliest intimation we have of Dietrich as the agent of fate who is willing to transgress society's conventions for those she adopts in her own heart. The part was much to her liking, though at this time she attacked the scene with the toughness of a hardbitten moll, not the resigned determination of a worldly sophisticate—not yet.

This, too, is the first time her name was linked publicly and usefully with a well-known man: Willi Forst, a twenty-six-year-old Viennese popular with both German and Austrian audiences, who had replaced the Berlin lead in the show. He and Dietrich found that their stage partnership enhanced their separate appeal by intensifying public curiosity about them as a couple. The first flavor of "celebrity" is generally a lingering one. Sieber appears to have been resigned to the professional opportunities which his wife was exploiting so advantageously, maybe reckoning that home life could still be a parallel, if separate, part of her professional life. Thus the pattern of her marital arrangements was established early and enduringly.

Dietrich had already appeared in the film *Sein grösster Bluff* (*His Greatest Bluff*: 1927), an extravagant farce about jewel robbers and mistaken identities in which she played a call girl with a wardrobe whose extensiveness showed her business to be a flourishing one. But with the success of *Broadway*, she and Willi Forst were rushed into *Café Electric* (1927), filmed in Vienna during August and September. She was still playing in *Broadway* by night.

Interestingly, she was not immediately cast in it as the industrialist's playgirl daughter who haunts the eponymous café and is seduced by Forst, its gigolo-in-residence. The producers, Sascha-Film, a subsidiary of UFA, first wanted to test her. Perhaps her pride made her resist; perhaps she was weary of continually playing the flirt; perhaps she was just tired, for she had already made two films that year and been kept busy in the long-running *Broadway*. What seems to have decided her in favor of the film was the test she finally consented to make with Forst, a love scene. Moreover, he had issued an ultimatum to the producers: having him in the film depended on their accepting Dietrich.

Once in the part, she played it in the overdrive manner of the American "flapper" girl soon to be popularized in MGM's *Dancing Daughters* cycle of comedies. She took every opportunity the script offered to display her legs and wore her smart wardrobe with the negligence of a rich girl accustomed to being spoiled with presents: she was called "quite provocative" by some of the critics. A

In *Sein grösster Bluff,* Dietrich played the part of a call girl who is on the make in more ways than one. She is pictured (*above*) with the film's director and star, Harry Piel. Sex-for-sale was a commonplace in 1920s Berlin. The mood of the times is reflected in a painting by Otto Dix, *Three Prostitutes in the Street* (*below*).

The American musical *Broadway*, in its 1927 Berlin incarnation, put Marlene on stage as a shapely chorine (she is at the left of the chorus line, *above*). When the show transferred to Vienna, Dietrich was given a more important role and came to the attention of the leading man, Willi Forst. On his insistence, she was paired with him in the film *Café Electric*, shot in Vienna during the run of *Broadway*. Once again Marlene played a flapper, this time the spoiled daughter of a rich industrialist (*below*).

curious story, which may be true, is told of her at this time—that Count Kolowrat, the gargantuan 360-pound head of Sascha-Film, mortally stricken with leukemia, begged Dietrich to come to his deathbed and display those famous legs for a last distraction. Legend has it that she coolly obliged. It would have been the sort of romantic gesture to appeal to her. Textual analysts of her second Hollywood film, *Dishonored*, suppose the incident to be commemorated obliquely—with a sardonic, not romantic, gloss put upon it—by a reference in the dialogue to Dietrich's being the widow of one "Captain Kolowrat."

It was in *Café Electric* that she was instructed by Igo Sym, one of her co-players, in a skill that she retained until relatively late in her career: the art of playing a musical saw. This curious instrument, the size and shape of a carpenter's saw, but without teeth, produced a seductively ululating sound when bent in an arc and stroked with a violin bow. The sound found some kind of echo in Dietrich's Teutonic soul, or else reminded her of her abandoned ambition to be a concert violinist on the more orthodox instrument. She even packed the saw in among the sparse baggage she was permitted to take to the war front in 1944 to entertain the troops.

Willi Forst went to Berlin to star in a romantic comedy, *Amor auf Ski* (*Love on Skis*), and Dietrich, returning to her own city and her family, achieved one of her most popular German film successes in *Prinzessin Olala* (*Princess Olala*: 1928) as a cocotte engaged to teach a virgin prince (played by Walter Rilla) all about the art of love. Her *real* love scenes are played with Hans Albers, a Reinhardt star with a burgeoning career. It was a good box-office combination. And Dietrich, with her hair in a fashionable shingle cut, her skirts shortened and her legs to the fore in numerous scenes that caught her supine, established herself as one of the best actresses at the time for combining seductiveness with self-mockery. She took her sense of enjoyment with her after hours, too, along with some of the wardrobe, to go nightclubbing in such *boîtes* as the Silhouette or the Weisse Rose, where show business rubbed shoulders with fashionable criminality.

It is amazing how she found the energy, never mind the time, to go into such stage productions as *Duell am Lido* or *Die Schule von Uznach*, both high-society farces. But by far her biggest success once again came from playing opposite another "masculine" woman. Margo Lion was the star of the revue *Es liegt in der Luft* (*It's in the Air*), a wickedly perverse satire of good times set in a Berlin department store where some lost children are reared in secret by the employees. So little does society change that the parents of the foundlings, on meeting them again, actually take their grandchildren to be their own offspring. Dietrich's wardrobe was her most lavish yet, especially one outfit of fox fur dyed scarlet, with rhinestone bracelets worn over arm's-length black gloves. One of her songs was a racy number with sexual innuendos about kleptomaniacs, and she once or twice borrowed the white top hat worn by her male singing partner. But the number that brought the house down was a duet with Margo Lion and Oskar Karlweis which left audiences chuckling as each of the ladies professed undying

love for the other, while hinting that each found the other an encumbrance in the pursuit of the same boyfriend (Karlweis).

Dietrich in those days had a far wider range of style than her later screen roles (or indeed her German films) suggest. She could go directly from a satirical musical like *It's in the Air* (which was eclipsed in popularity only by another show that was running across town, the Bertolt Brecht–Kurt Weill *Dreigroschenoper*) into "serious" plays like Shaw's *Misalliance* (as Hypatia) and *Back to Methuselah* (as Eve). Such plays showed she could sustain a long dramatic role with flair and variation. Alfred Kerr, the *doyen* of Berlin theater critics, noted that she could "sit apart" from a cast that was perhaps less distinguished than the play needed and still hold the attention of the house just by doing nothing. It was this "presence" that the movie cameras of Hollywood were to make famous.

The provocative vamp that was lying in wait is visible in prototype in her next film, *Ich küsse ihre Hand, Madame* (*I Kiss Your Hand, Madame*: 1929), written and directed by Robert Land, who no doubt wanted a quick follow-up to the success of his *Prinzessin Olala*. Shot in studios in Berlin and Paris, it was a part-talkie— "the first sound film [shown] in Hamburg," according to one critic. It featured Dietrich as a society woman who has no sooner got her divorce papers than she falls in love with a man whom she takes to be a Russian nobleman. (He is played by Harry Liedtke, a matinée idol of the day, whose songs in the film were later revoiced by Richard Tauber.) He turns out to be a head waiter: a typical plot device. And then he turns out to be a real White Russian aristocrat: an even more typical plot and rather truer to reality than one might expect, insofar as there were then in Berlin many once rich and well-connected Russians who had fled from the Revolution and settled there without their fortunes.

Some critics looked down their noses, understandably, at this fricassee of clichés, but Dietrich received invariably enthusiastic mentions. "Her cool, ladylike appearance is evidence of exceptional cinematic talent," Hans Sahl wrote in Berlin's *Montag Morgen*.[8] An anonymous critic in the *Hamburger Anzeiger* went further: "And now we come to what makes the film finally so indisputably piquant. It presents . . . a medium-blonde woman, with somewhat tired eyelids and a beautifully feminine mouth: Marlene Dietrich. She is, in short, the 'Madame' whose hand is kissed. Her performance is not bad. . . . To have to be erotic and yet have style, to have to be 'Madame' and yet be able to run off with other men: this is a new type of woman, if you believe Robert Land."[9] One certainly sees the genesis of the great vamp she was soon to create as Dietrich alternatively lures her man on by her coy acceptance of his kisses, then pushes him away with ladylike discretion when he is too importunate. She is forever patting her hair like a coquette preparing herself for seduction and then, when betrayed, powdering her face with a ruthless hand and applying the full war paint of pursuit, though she still lacks the will as well as the means to humiliate her fickle lover with the predatory thoroughness of the true *femme fatale*. Her face is gaunter, too, than in her earlier films, and those famous hollows below the cheekbones, which it was

Dietrich's legs were on prominent display in *Prinzessin Olala*, a light film comedy in which she played opposite the Reinhardt star Hans Albers.

In the late 1920s, Dietrich successfully combined careers on stage and on screen. Among her theatrical hits was *Es liegt in der Luft,* a musical in which she co-starred with Margo Lion and Oskar Karlweis (*right*). In a Reinhardt production of Shaw's *Misalliance* (*below*), Dietrich was cast in the role of Hypatia. The camera caught her leaning provocatively against the wall in a pose that would become a Dietrich trademark.

At about the same time she appeared as the leading lady in the film *Ich küsse ihre Hand, Madame* (*opposite page*). The famous hollows below the cheekbones begin to be evident. The film was mostly silent but included some songs recorded off-camera by the celebrated tenor Richard Tauber. The inset photo shows Tauber (with monocle), Dietrich and two unidentified studio executives.

falsely rumored had been cosmetically induced by a dental operation after her arrival in Hollywood, are already giving her expression its concave allure.

But some critics felt it reminded them of another and more celebrated face. Hanns Lustig wrote in Berlin's *Tempo*, "Why has she been given the *coiffure* of the Swedish star? Why has she been put into Garbo's clothes? True enough, this German girl (who has really not all that many German characteristics) has a similar and curiously alluring expression of immobility and indolence. . . . [But] why not seek out the personality of the woman herself, without foisting a foreign one upon her?"[10] Another magazine even featured a split-cover illustration: Dietrich on one half of the page, Garbo on the other.

Almost as soon as she had finished celebrating Christmas with Rudi and Heidede, she was rushed into another film by Kurt (later to become, in his Hollywood days, "Curtis") Bernhardt. He had confessed himself captivated by seeing Dietrich as Shaw's Hypatia a few months earlier.

Die Frau, nach der man sich sehnt (*The Woman One Longs For*: 1929) anticipates one of Dietrich's later films even more strongly because much of the action is set on an express train, bound not for Shanghai, but for the Riviera. Dietrich "materializes" out of her lover's compartment like a phantom *femme fatale*, without background and almost without substance, and seduces a newly wedded husband with one look just as his timorous wife has repulsed his honeymoon advances. Her "Stascha" is a destroyer of men who casts them off the minute she tires of them. Dietrich was now sufficiently conscious of her celebrity to be a little troublesome about the way she was usually presented. Curtis later told the biographer Charles Higham that she was worried about her *retroussé* nose and balked at doing profile shots. When required to talk to someone on her right or left, she simply swiveled an eyeball in the direction indicated and "talked" to the camera. "It drove Fritz Kortner [the male lead] crazy," said Bernhardt.

Kortner shoots Dietrich at the end of this silent drama: it was her first experience of the narcissistic pleasure which an imitation of death can induce in a performer. A mortal fate is one that some screen personalities can accept (and others positively demand) since their romantic extinction seems to complete an audience's unconscious involvement with them and the character they play more satisfyingly than if they survive to sin another day. "From this film on," Manfred George recalled in his memoirs, but surely a little late in his dating of the event, "she was becoming known in film circles. . . . Already one saw the large eyes . . . the smile which means so many things, the lure of the mouth and the softly curling hair. . . . Here was the illumination of her personality, even if not yet the final breakthrough."[11]

In March or April 1929, the young English actor Robert Irvine arrived at Berlin's Staaken film studios to play a role in a silent melodrama entitled *Das Schiff der verlorenen Menschen* (*Ship of Lost Souls*: 1929), which was being shot by the French director Maurice Tourneur. It was a trite story: a lady pilot crash-lands in the ocean near a mystery ship, gets picked up and then has to run the gauntlet of

Critics began to complain that Dietrich was being made into a carbon copy of Garbo. The resemblances are apparent in stills from two films of the same date: *Die Frau, nach der man sich sehnt*, starring Dietrich, and *The Kiss*, starring Garbo (inset).

the smugglers, hijackers and criminals who comprise its crew. The makers probably hoped to give the potboiler at least a visual impressiveness: they built a full-scale reconstruction of the hulk 100 feet tall and, according to publicity statistics, 800,000 nails were holding it all together. Just to create the wind that lashed the surface of the ocean "tank" cost 300 marks a day. On the whole, German critics remained unimpressed. "One single raging brawl," was how Hans Sahl dismissed the storm (and the plot) in his *Montag Morgen* notice; but he conceded that Dietrich was magnificent to look at in her aviatrix's leather flying suit or fleeing in borrowed male clothing through the chiaroscuro lighting of a labyrinth of companionways.[12] Irvine played a young American doctor, forced to make the voyage against his will, who befriends the glamorous flotsam and saves both her honor and her life. It is to him that we owe the earliest, indeed the *only* eyewitness description of Dietrich at work just prior to her international stardom.

Writing in the British magazine *Film Weekly* in 1931, just a year after Dietrich's incredibly swift ascent in the Hollywood firmament, Irvine recalled that he heard the lady in the German studios even before he met her. From her dressing room came the slightly bizarre sound of a Viennese waltz played on a musical saw. Then Tourneur introduced him to "a girl in a black tailor-made suit, collar and tie"—it must have been Dietrich's ordinary day clothes, as she wears no such outfit in the film—with "her hair scraped off her forehead and the most provocative tip-tilted nose I have ever seen."[13] Besides the musical saw, she possessed a portable phonograph, which she was in the habit of carting around with her wherever she went, into the Berlin cafés as well as the film studios, in order to play the American songs and dance music she felt fitted her ambience (in particular she liked Irving Berlin's "Always"). But she also loved Debussy and Ravel—her classical education had clearly not been wasted—and she played them too for Irvine. Probably taking pity on such a good-looking young Englishman alone in Berlin, she took him home to the apartment in the Kaiserallee. The mood was even more relaxed when the two of them went out dancing—Sieber was working nights and apparently was well used to his wife's liking for the bright lights.

To Irvine, she appeared carefree, a trifle fey, devoid of much sense of responsibility and totally indifferent to other people's opinion or conventional obligations—in short, rather like the character of Sally Bowles, who became the pleasure-loving spirit of interwar Berlin for another young Englishman in town, Christopher Isherwood. The one thing she was overly conscious about was that "ski-tip" nose, which Irvine, on more than one occasion, caught her trying to "improve"—whatever this may mean. There was nothing at all in her character, as far as he could see, of the *jeune fille*: she was "entirely cosmopolitan," though not at all "pushful or aggressive." And she spoke "excellent English." "A good trouper," was Irvine's (typically English gentleman's) verdict on her; but he noted, significantly, that "even then she was an actress of note in Berlin."

She was good enough to survive even a rank bad picture, which her next one turned out to be. Its recurrent changes of title were ominous—from *One Night of*

Das Schiff der verlorenen Menschen embroiled Dietrich as an American aviatrix in a ship full of unsavory characters. Here, however, garbed in the trousers that would soon become another trademark, she has merely to cope with a tabby cat.

By 1929, Marlene Dietrich was enough of a personage to be photographed in her apartment in Berlin's Kaiserallee. The heavy, bourgeois decor hardly matches the actress's studiously sultry poses.

Love, it became *From the Diary of a Seducer*, then *Love Letter* and *Night of Love*, until finally, and disastrously, it was released as *Gefahren der Brautzeit* (*Dangers of the Engagement Period*: 1929). Understandably irritated by the pretentious solemnity of a title with undertones of a sex-hygiene film, contemporary critics were merciless. "Simply a self-indulgent 'woman's movie,'" scoffed the Munich *Neue Zeitung*'s reviewer, "G. F.," "about an amorous baron [Willi Forst again] who goes from bed to bed while one girl after another is presented to us in a state of half-undress. . . . The one thing we wait for in vain are the dangers of the engagement period."[14] In this silent melodrama Dietrich was the woman seduced, not the *provocatrice*, who falls victim to the baron on a railway train taking her to her fiancé. The fiancé turns out to be the baron's best friend. This time it is the penitent male who does the decent thing and shoots himself. Yet among the caustic comments—"the sort of kitsch production which once threatened discredit to the German cinema" was typical—some critics, like the reviewer "R. E." in Berlin's *8-Uhr Morgenblatt*, exempted the "prominent players . . . Marlene Dietrich, Ernst Stahl-Nachbaur and Willi Forst," placing Dietrich at the top of the list of honorable (or at least pardonable) exceptions.

That this wasn't just a courtesy ranking is confirmed by the remarks of no less distinguished a critic than Lotte Eisner. Frau Eisner, later a power at the Paris *cinemathèque* and, until her death in 1983, regarded as one of the most authoritative writers on pre-Hitler German cinema, made her comments in Berlin's *Film-Kurier* well after the film's release—and indeed after Dietrich had left Germany for "an engagement in Hollywood far away from us." It may be true that distance lent enchantment to the review, but Frau Eisner does not hesitate to see the film as "an attempt to create a frame for Marlene Dietrich"—very much of a "star vehicle," therefore.[15] The screenwriters (Wassermann and Schlee) "show us a woman who materializes mysteriously and sadly in a railway compartment . . . a night of love gained through a railroad accident . . . the sudden flight of the unknown beauty." Frau Eisner pays special attention to the role of photography in "creating" a Dietrich who is "charming and alluring in her blend of mysterious behavior and peculiar passivity, her lovely face overshadowed by a presentiment of tragedy. . . . Schaffer [László Schaffer, the lighting cameraman] takes pains to emphasize her expression to bring out a figure at dusk in a railway compartment, illuminated by guttering oil lamps. He does not seek to achieve virtuoso contrasts of brightness and deep shadow, but a mixture of the tones in between."

This knowledgeable historian makes us feel that the image of Dietrich created out of atmosphere and lighting effects is already present—and this well before Josef von Sternberg, her psychological mentor and the man who imposed "his" vision of her on the screen and the world, had even arrived in Berlin.

These films with Dietrich were made quickly, in weeks rather than months, though the adoption of directly recorded sound by German studios from 1930, or thereabouts, was to slow down the production process. (Only one of her films, *I Kiss Your Hand, Madame*, had been released with a song-and-music track in the

Dietrich's last "minor" German film was a silent melodrama, *Gefahren der Brautzeit*, in which she again played opposite Willi Forst. Cameraman László Schaffer's lighting helped to delineate a Dietrich "charming and alluring in her blend of mysterious behavior and charming passivity."

46

manner of *The Jazz Singer*.) But her singing voice was already distinctive and well known: not only from her stage musicals, but on phonograph recordings she made for Telefunken. Two numbers especially, *Peter* and *Jonny*, were to become classics. Recordings could easily be fitted in between films; and it increased her reputation as an entertainer—and provided useful additional income.

Dietrich had no film commitments in the summer of 1929 and accepted a stage role with alacrity—this time as the female lead. The part was ideal. *Zwei Kravatten* (*Two Neckties*) was a satire on the idle rich of America who knew money could buy anything, but bought most when love came along as part of it. The score was composed by Mischa Spoliansky (who had done *It's in the Air*) with book and lyrics by the Expressionist playwright Georg Kaiser. Dietrich played a rich American girl who falls in love with a lottery winner—actually a waiter who has changed clothes with a fugitive gangster (the "imposture" motif was inescapable in German entertainment of the period) and sails for America with him in tow. They go through Chicago gangland and an engagement in Miami before true love wins—or almost, for when the waiter reclaims his German fiancée, he finds she has inherited several million more dollars than his erstwhile American love! Hans Albers played the waiter. The musical was a perfect showcase for Dietrich's by now well-tested ability to display, by turns, flirtatiousness, world-weariness, irony and cynicism, and she delivered Kaiser's hard-centered lyrics parodying the capitalist system with a well-trained attack that gained added emphasis when Wall Street collapsed just a few weeks after *Two Neckties* opened at the Komödie Theater on September 1, 1929, to universally enthusiastic notices.

One of the scenes portrayed Dietrich leaning against the rail of a transatlantic liner wearing an expression which one member of the audience that night characterized as "cold disdain." It is possible that Josef von Sternberg was merely projecting on to her the customary view that he himself took of the world, in whichever part of it he happened to be. But certainly it made a vivid impression on him—so much so that he was to reproduce that pose of Dietrich's in film after film, in different lights and shadows, against different backgrounds, as if it possessed the miraculous power of an epiphany. He was to be accused years later of simply using Dietrich as the principal romantic prop in his inventory of erotic effects. Untrue: but he certainly sensed the suggestive insolence emanating from her when she was "propped up."

The impression of her in *Two Neckties*, as she feigned indifference to Hans Albers at the start of their shipboard romance, fortuitously corresponded to exactly what Von Sternberg, who had arrived in Berlin towards the end of August 1929 to make a prestigious sound film for UFA, demanded of the players he was accustomed to dragooning through his previous Hollywood productions. It was nothing short of a willingness by them to project his own attitude to life. "I gave her nothing that she did not already have," he said, when he came to write his memoirs thirty-five years later. "What I did was to dramatize her attributes and make them visible for all to see; though, as there were perhaps too many, I

Without any film commitments for the moment, Dietrich returned to the stage in a musical satire entitled *Zwei Kravatten*, which opened at the Komödie Theater on September 1, 1929. She played a rich American girl who falls in love with a lottery winner (Hans Albers). It was in this production that Josef von Sternberg first saw the performer whose destiny he was to shape so enduringly.

concealed some."[16] Obedience, humility, self-abasement were also things he demanded from others; like many another autocrat, they were the ones he most conspicuously lacked himself.

As this is the man whose name was about to be inextricably linked with Marlene Dietrich's extraordinary transformation into a world-famous star, Von Sternberg deserves deeper study. He had been born plain Jonas Sternberg in Vienna, in 1894. The "von" in his name was acquired in Hollywood. An obscure producer added it to the credits on the screen for the sake of "symmetry," or so the story goes. When critics jeered at the pretentiousness it represented, Sternberg belligerently adopted it and very easily assimilated its aristocratic nuances into his own autocratic bearing. He had first gone to America at the age of seven, when his father, Moses, sent for his family to leave their ghetto home in Vienna and join him in New York. For obscure reasons, they returned to Europe three years later; and Jonas (who soon changed his name to Josef) did not return to America until he was fourteen—but this time for good. He quit formal schooling at sixteen and took a variety of casual jobs, including one as a clerk in a millinery store and another as an invoicer in a lace warehouse. It is easy to see a connection between this work and his later love of exotic decoration in his films. But in fact he already possessed an uncommonly good eye for viewing the world, since the great museums and art galleries in New York and elsewhere, where he resorted for warmth and shelter as much as esthetic stimulation, bombarded him with examples of some of the best masters of light and shade. Von Sternberg later became one of the most knowledgeable art collectors in Hollywood.

By 1911, he was working in New York repairing damaged film prints; his contempt for the crude content of most of the films he handled caught their producers' attention and won him promotion as a "film doctor," offering practical advice to scores of small-time independent filmmakers. After World War I—he served in the Signal Corps, making training films—he made his way to Hollywood, working off and on as an assistant director, but keeping to himself, living alone, feeding his imagination more frequently than his stomach on an eclectic diet of the classics.

In many ways, Josef von Sternberg resembled that other celebrated autodidact and "dictator," Charles Chaplin. Both men eventually wrote memoirs that are in fact piteous recollections of their impoverished backgrounds, as well as arrogant testimony to the authors' self-importance—exemplified in the choice they made of stilted phraseology and esoteric vocabulary. Von Sternberg's book is a tale of contempt as well as suffering. He extended his disdain of convention even into the very index whose alphabetized sections are like a surreal joke played on the reader. Under the letter "C" one finds: "Capek, Karl; capital of filmdom; Capra, Frank; carnal; Carné, Marcel; cart before the horse; *Case of Lena Smith, The*; catalyst; *caveat emptor*;" etc., and under "E" such listings as "ear-wax extractors; Earl of Rochester," etc. One supposes the publisher told him an index was essential and Von Sternberg, nobody's minion, disdainfully served this one up.

Josef von Sternberg, c. 1930.
The picture below shows him
at work and wearing his
customary expression of
world-weary disdain.

With Chaplin, he shared the autodidact's delight in unearthing the exotic. He, too, was a combination of tyrant and bohemian such as Chaplin quickly became. He was wont to offset his small physique—another thing he had in common with the antic Charlie—by wearing exotic costumes: fur coats, cloaks, turbans, riding breeches, velvet berets, etc. He had a full head of hair carefully trained to dangle over his forehead. His deep-set eyes and the sardonic mustache he cultivated gave him an Oriental look—or a Mephisthophelean one, according to one's view of the man. And he adopted Chaplin's own working method, which was one of imposing endless repetition on all concerned until the effect he sought in a scene had refined itself and been achieved. He gave precise orders and permitted no deviation in the playing of a role. Von Sternberg had got his first chance as director when a British stage actor, George K. Arthur, anxious to subsidize a star role for himself in a Hollywood film, approached him for suggestions. With a meager budget and no established names, he shot a story of waterfront derelicts entitled *The Salvation Hunters* (1925), using locations among the docks of San Pedro Bay. The subject and his austerely poetic treatment were novelties for that time. Von Sternberg described it in terms that sound like a parody of the "art film," though he possibly intended it to express his scorn for the commercially tainted Hollywood product. "Three derelicts live on a mud scow, from which circumstances and environment release them after poetically conceived tribulations."

Chaplin saw it and, maybe sympathizing with its anti-Hollywood bias, at once engaged Von Sternberg and assigned him to direct Edna Purviance (Chaplin's mistress), in a film called *The Sea Gull*. Chaplin was possibly in search of proletarian humanism—such as Italian neo-realism would rediscover in the postwar cinema in 1945—and realized that his own reputation for comedy would work against the film's serious reception by the public. But instead he got a film filled with abstract patterns of sea, sand and nets; after one screening, he consigned it to his vaults from which it never again emerged (and is unlikely still to exist, since the insurance claim that Chaplin typically made for his disappointment almost certainly enforced its destruction).

What Chaplin had accurately sensed in Von Sternberg was the fascination which the female held for both men as an object of desire. No doubt he secretly hoped that Edna Purviance's sex appeal would be enhanced by the care that Von Sternberg lavished on her. But he overlooked, or chose to ignore, one basic difference between them. Chaplin adored women. While not averse to carnal satisfaction, he made them overimaginatively into ideals of womanhood. Von Sternberg, on the contrary, disdained women. There is no evidence of his ever having sexual relations with his female stars (a fair consensus doubted it). He preferred to emphasize the female's destructive nature. Chaplin was the "undisputed sovereign of comic humiliation," in Von Sternberg's words. Von Sternberg, in turn, was to become the lord and master of erotic humiliation. And in Marlene Dietrich he found his most celebrated agent to inflict that humiliation.

Yet "find" is not the word: "shape" is better. As John Baxter, one of his best critics, put it: Von Sternberg's talent was to "select from the work of others the elements he wanted to use." Among these elements were, first, Dietrich's own nature; second, films which she had already made which reflected aspects of it; and third, Von Sternberg's own specifications for the "visionary woman" which in his imagination he had formulated, using images created by his predecessors in erotic perversity—Baudelaire, Beardsley, Goya, Huysmans and Félicien Rops.

These were the names he evoked when he arrived in Berlin with his wife, Riza Royce von Sternberg. He was there at the invitation of UFA's production chief, Erich Pommer, to guide the German film industry's greatest male star, Emil Jannings, through his first sound film. Jannings had insisted on having Von Sternberg, who had previously directed his Hollywood silent film, *The Last Command* (1928). The two despots suited each other to an extent that neither would bring himself to admit. Von Sternberg took a cynical but frequently just view of the actor's ego, which fortifies itself in proportion to the pains inflicted on it: "I suffer, therefore I am." Jannings was a most receptive spirit: this burly figure (capable, though, of many delicate physical shadings in his performance) reveled in the agonies of characters whose destiny was to be publicly humiliated—the groveling of the erstwhile high and mighty, the demotion of the vain and powerful, all were meat and drink to Jannings. He grew fat on it. Von Sternberg supped at the same dish, but in a more refined way. The theme is served up with many variations in his memoirs, from the sexual humiliation inflicted on Viennese prostitutes by packs of fierce urchins who tossed their skirts up, through personal humiliations like the charity-chest clothes little Josef was forced to wear, to the best humiliation of all, which was the artistic abasement of a famous star before his or her unrelenting director.

The Von Sternbergs moved into a Berlin apartment owned by the theater director Erwin Piscator. Von Sternberg liked even his temporary domicile to be "in fashion"—back home in Hollywood he owned one of the earliest steel-frame houses designed by the German émigré architect Richard Neutra, shaped with typical bombast in the S-form of the master's initial. His sado-masochistic itch was probably gratifyingly exacerbated by the power he knew he could command at UFA.

Von Sternberg's own power at the Paramount studios in Hollywood had waxed and waned in the previous three or four years: he was alternately revered and reviled by the front office according to the sums of money that his films made or lost. Some, like *Underworld* (1927), made a lot and gave the American gangster cycle a new lease of violent life; others, like *The Case of Lena Smith* (1929), did not recover even their cost. But Paramount was preeminently a "directors' studio," just as much as MGM was a "producers' outfit," and a man who deliberately set out to impose himself on the set-up by force of will—in Von Sternberg's case, he made himself hated by virtually everyone—enjoyed grudging artistic pardon even if a movie (or maybe two) lacked strength at the box office.

Von Sternberg had been given extraordinarily wide powers by UFA, which was counting both on his advanced knowledge of directing talkies—Germany lagged behind Hollywood at this time—and on the Paramount connection to give the Jannings film (whatever it might be) an *entrée* to the American market. He used these powers even before he arrived to veto UFA's suggestion of a film about Rasputin—a "story that permitted no speculation about its outcome" did nothing for him, he declared. The property finally selected was *Professor Unrat* (an untranslatable title meaning literally "Professor Garbage"). It was a very odd choice, not just because it was a novel which had been written as long ago as 1905, by Heinrich Mann, but also because it was an attack on the pretensions of the German bourgeoisie—and the owner of UFA, Alfred Hugenberg, was a celebrated representative of that very class, a financier, newspaper magnate and supporter of the National Socialist movement that was soon to put Hitler in power. The story satirized Hugenberg's own values (and those of his paper's readership). It was about a pompous high-school teacher, ruined by his erotic fascination with the star of the local cabaret, who then (as the book has it) comes back to town a hardened cynic and opens a casino where it is his turn to ruin the community that spurned him.

But politics didn't interest Von Sternberg at all. He saw no difficulty in limiting himself to the section of the story describing the self-destruction of the professor, and even inspired a new ending which further curtailed the novel's polemical thrust by having the professor expire from heartbreak and mortification in his own classroom. This prospect set Jannings licking his chops.

Der blaue Engel (*The Blue Angel*: 1930), as it was renamed, was an important production. Rivalry for a part in it was intense. The actress cast in the leading female role would become an international name, if all went well. But who would she be?

The story has grown up that Dietrich was the last to be considered. This is quite untrue. She was among the first to be proposed—by Karl Vollmöller, who was UFA's go-between with Paramount, and her nomination was supported by Carl Zuckmayer, poet, playwright and eventual co-author of the scenario. But it is true that the rejection of her didn't take much time, either: it was instantaneous. "Not that whore!" the studio's production chief, Erich Pommer, reportedly bawled. Party politics then broke out, with everyone running their "favorite daughter" for the job, while UFA went through the motions of a general talent hunt. Von Sternberg at this time preferred Brigitte Helm, star of *Metropolis* and *The Loves of Jeanne Ney*, but a pending appendectomy ruled her out. Heinrich Mann, backed by Pommer, suggested Trude Hesterberg, an actress and a star of cabaret and revue. Lucie Mannheim, a distinguished pillar of the Volksbühne Theater, was strongly tipped and even got as far as a screen test for which she brought along a pianist, Friedrich Holländer, and a specially written song—though as yet there were no songs planned for the *Blue Angel* scenario. Typically, Von Sternberg rejected the actress but kept the pianist and suggested that he revise his lyric, making it more

Der blaue Engel, the film which "made" Marlene Dietrich overnight, was originally conceived primarily as a vehicle for the actor Emil Jannings. He is shown here on the set with director Von Sternberg looking unusually contented.

cynical and above all retaining the line about "falling in love again." A persistent report had the actress Käthe Haack actually signed for the part, though she was thirty-eight. Von Sternberg's own account of the search reads like the memoirs of a pasha asked to select a favorite lady from other people's harems: "One had the necessary eyes, another a graceful posture, one legs that weren't knock-kneed, and still another a voice that promised devilry, but I could not see how half a dozen different women could be made to play one part."

He is said to have seen a flatly lit picture of Dietrich in a casting directory which his assistant had passed over to him with the dismissive comment, "All right from the rear, but don't we need a face as well?", and he is also said to have witnessed the lady herself, playing her musical saw, at a supper party at the Reinhardt mansion. If so, he was not inspired by her on these occasions.

It was not until he went to the *Two Neckties* musical, in order to check the suitability of Hans Albers and Rosa Valetti, who were in the show and already almost certain to be cast for *The Blue Angel*, that his eye caught Dietrich in her striking pose of imperious indifference. He was able to see the suggestion of her other physical attributes as a wind-machine blew her red gown seductively close to the contours of her limbs. But we may be sure that what Von Sternberg really saw was the image that was already in his own mind's eye. "Here was not only a model who had been designed by Rops, but Toulouse-Lautrec would have turned a couple of handsprings had he laid eyes on her. Her appearance was ideal: what she did with it was something else again. That would be my concern."[17]

It is a matter for speculation—but, from what we know of the man, well-based speculation—that Von Sternberg was *already* transforming *The Blue Angel* from a vehicle for Jannings into an artistic opportunity for himself to create in the flesh the woman he fantasized in his mind. He must have realized that the film's impact depended on the exciting new vision it would offer of destructive womanhood—otherwise, it would simply be an illustrative essay on the downfall of a school tyrant.

Dietrich's reaction to his offering her the role intrigued him even more; she showed no elation whatsoever. She sat opposite him at the UFA studios in a heliotrope winter suit, with hat, gloves and fur: a study in ladylike apathy, the disdain that he had found so seductive on the stage now modulated into mere uninterest. Perhaps she feared rejection. She had been turned down flat the previous year by Pabst, who was casting the role of Lulu in *Pandora's Box*, with the crushing comment (according to Louise Brooks, who got the role) that "one sexy look [from Dietrich] and the picture would become a burlesque." The character of Lola-Lola in *The Blue Angel* was inspired by Lulu: her name had been "doubled" by the cynical Von Sternberg in order to make her "twice as sexy." It may have suggested a double rebuff to Dietrich. She was certainly a well-known film actress, as the chronicle of her career up to 1930 testifies. And though she may have later said that she made no picture before *The Blue Angel*, it is to be presumed that she meant "no picture that counted." But even this is untrue. Some of her

pictures counted for a lot in the estimation of critics and box office. What perhaps counted against her in the first round of "possibles" was the typecasting she had suffered in many of her films: she was usually the obvious coquette rather than a mysterious *femme fatale*. In her last few films, this latter aspect of her *persona* was emerging thanks to understanding directors and cameramen, but it is significant that Von Sternberg saw its potential in her stage rather than in her film work. She also lacked the social connections of, say, Lucie Mannheim or Brigitte Helm, which gave those actresses a higher status in the snobbish Berlin film world.

It could be, however, that she understood the man in front of her all too well and found his autocratic demeanor suggesting vaguely, yet reassuringly, the childhood discipline of home life where "one does not show one's feelings, it is bad manners."

There seems to have been an element of self-abasement in her lack of enthusiasm as she told Von Sternberg three "home truths" about herself: that she could not act, that the press treated her badly, that her last three films had been badly received. This was far from the truth, as we have seen, but for Von Sternberg this unsolicited confession was a novel experience. No one to whom he had offered a starring role before had taken so much trouble to tell him of their failures. In short, either by design or not, Dietrich adopted just the line in malleable passivity calculated to intrigue a man who—as his wife bitterly insisted later—had been seduced by the possibility of making this woman over into "a new and exciting female."

Still showing little enthusiasm, Dietrich borrowed an outsize spangled costume from the UFA wardrobe department—Von Sternberg had to pin it up against her body—and launched into one of the songs she had prepared. She endowed it with all the unconcern of someone feeling it was a waste of time. After "You're the cream in my coffee," which she did in English, she sang a German song composed by Peter Kreuder, who was to be the film's musical director: "Why cry when you say goodbye to someone/There's someone else around the corner." Von Sternberg hated making the test. Its utilitarian nature did not enable him to create the German *Stimmung*, those vibrations of mood composed largely out of lighting effects which correspond to the state of the player's soul, and were the "signature" look of the old High German cinema. Yet, as he instructed her, Dietrich came to life. She performed with exemplary ease. She was so cool about it all that she never even asked to see the test—and her very indifference flattered her future mentor.

The UFA executives were shocked. They viewed the test and howled down Von Sternberg's nominee—just as Mauritz Stiller's associates had vociferously opposed *his* selection of an untried and unknown Greta Garbo for a major film, and for the same reason. Each man had an ideal vision of womanhood that did not correspond to the view that his associates had of the specific example displayed. But Von Sternberg exercised his contractual right to cast the picture. A weary Pommer, anxious to get the film under way, supported him, and only Emil

Jannings "muttered in a hollow voice that would have brought credit to Cassandra that I would rue the day."

Von Sternberg boasted later that Dietrich offered "not the slightest resistance . . . to my domination." Yet it was only the truth. She put herself totally in his hands. And he proceeded to suppress the very characteristics that had been dominant in her earlier roles on stage and screen—her vitality, humor, mischievousness, warmth of heart and the Berlin equivalent of the street-wise waif bent on survival. There now appeared a *femme fatale* who was cynical, disdainful and incapable of showing sympathy with human suffering or remorse for being the cause of it: the distaff side of Von Sternberg's own nature.

The really shocking thing about Lola-Lola, star of the Blue Angel cabaret, is not her deliberate ruin of the pompous burgher who has become infatuated with her—it is the way she stands aside and watches him destroy himself. She remains impassive as he abandons social status for sexual enslavement, symbolized by padlocks in place of cufflinks and a collar like a slave's neckband on the clown's outfit he dons. His wail of grief across the footlights from the depths of his humiliation as he sees Lola-Lola taking a new lover transposes the rooster's crow of "Cock-a-doodle-doo" into an echo of "Cuck-ol-ded." It was a typical piece of invention by Von Sternberg, which fed Jannings's masochism: the latter decreed that only rotten eggs were to be broken over his head as the humiliated man is anointed in a final defilement. The novel contains no such scene.

It's true that Dietrich tantalizes her lover. She puffs face powder provocatively into his beard and lets her lacy underwear float down from her upstairs dressing room and land on his upturned face as (we suppose) he glimpses her private parts. Heinrich Mann told Jannings that the film's success would depend on "the naked thighs of Marlene Dietrich." Not a tactful observation to such a man: but a reasonably accurate forecast in view of the way that the notorious shot of Dietrich seated on a barrel, lolling invitingly back in her cutaway skirt, her black suspenders tightly stretched against her pale legs, has become one of the best-known erotic icons in cinema history. Lola-Lola was sex incarnate. Yet for most of the film, Dietrich remains physically and emotionally detached about it all. She stands on those "provocative legs," as Siegfried Kracauer called them, and regards the spectacle her victim is making of himself coolly and egoistically. Von Sternberg does not exploit their relationship: he simply depicts the physical servility of Jannings, who is forever dropping abjectly on his knees in front of her to pick up erotic postcards, or helping her roll on her stockings. Lola-Lola remains uninvolved, more narcissist than *femme fatale*. What she keeps falling in love with is her own image. No wonder that song has such a damnably introspective ring!

There is an odd, seldom-noticed discrepancy between the German version of Friedrich Holländer's famous song and its translation in the English version. In German, Lola-Lola's song goes, "Ich bin von Kopf bis Fuss/Auf Liebe eingestellt" ("From head to toe/I'm made for love," and it continues "For that's

Lola-Lola and Professor Rath celebrate their wedding while Friedrich Holländer provides some music in the background. Holländer's bittersweet songs contributed importantly to *The Blue Angel*'s success.

Opposite: Lola-Lola has begun to wind the hapless professor around her index finger.

my world/ And nothing else at all"). But in English, in which the song is more familiar, the lyrics are far more heartless: "Falling in love again/Never wanted to/What am I to do?/Can't help it." In short, it becomes the siren song of an automaton temptress, a mechanical Circe which is set in motion by the perverse circuitry that has replaced her heart.

That this was Von Sternberg's concept, and no one else's, was confirmed in an affidavit sworn by Dietrich thirty years later, when the director was about to sue Twentieth Century-Fox for infringing his rights in the original film by remaking it with Mai Britt and Curt Jurgens in the leading roles. (The suit was eventually dropped.) Dietrich testified that Jannings had told her that if she played the role in the heartless fashion decreed by Von Sternberg, "she would be through with films in Germany, for no one would ever again employ her." He told her it was "a completely unsympathetic character and not at all [the one] he had seen when he was deciding to make the film." The actress further testified that he maliciously tried to incite her to disregard their director's instructions. It seems that Jannings's chronic suspiciousness had turned him into a monster of jealousy and antagonism. He it was who had come to rue the day Dietrich was cast, as he saw his own prestigious debut in the talkies being subverted into a showcase for the actress. During the shooting of one scene, his anger got the better of him and he

turned his discovery of Lola-Lola with her new lover into an excuse for assaulting Dietrich so forcibly that the crew had to separate them and she was compelled to wear a velvet neckband to hide the bruises that night when she appeared on stage in *Two Neckties*, in which she was performing concurrently with the filming. Von Sternberg was certainly testing her *Hausfrau* energy!

Jannings sulked in his dressing room, rage and tears further bloating his huge face. He then besieged Von Sternberg, demanding that Dietrich's role be abridged and his own expanded. In vain. However the film might be reshaped, the emphasis of its interest would remain on the destroyer, not her victim. Von Sternberg had the right to the final cut. He had additionally forearmed himself by bringing his own editor, Sam Winston, over from Hollywood to cut both the English and German versions. In fact, Von Sternberg edited all his own films, though for craft union reasons he had to forgo any screen credit. The notorious pleasure he took in compelling players to repeat a scene ad infinitum had its rationale; for if they couldn't (or wouldn't) do what he wanted on the set, then he had the power and an abundance of raw material to make them appear to do it for him in the cutting rooms. He is said to have put Dietrich through her famous siren song some 200 times until the Weintraub Syncopators, the Berlin group who were engaged as the musicians at the Blue Angel café, were as exhausted as she was.

It is impossible to say if, or how much, Von Sternberg had fallen in love with his star: the likelihood is that in such an egoistic man, the beloved's face was only a reflecting mirror for his own narcissistic vision. In the films they were soon to make together in Hollywood, Von Sternberg nearly always included a character who bore so close a physical resemblance to himself that he might have been taken for a double of the director. He thus gained an erotic satisfaction by proxy without having to suffer the artistic pains of the actor. If Dietrich's husband was uncomfortable about his wife's relationship with her director, he characteristically kept his silence. Not so Riza Royce von Sternberg, who abruptly quit Berlin in the middle of shooting; later she interpreted her husband's attachment to Dietrich as the act of someone seeking neither power nor love, but masochistic satisfaction. "Before he worked with [Dietrich] his films were presented with the legend 'A Josef von Sternberg Production,'" she wrote John Kobal. "After he was in Marlene's hooks, his films advertised Marlene Dietrich in big letters and his name was small and insignificant underneath."[18]

We have already seen that the characteristic "Dietrich face" had been latent in the camerawork of some of her better photographed films. A thoroughgoing cosmetic remodeling of it came with her Hollywood contract: but even in *The Blue Angel*, amendments were made with the materials to hand. Chief of these was lighting. Frequently Von Sternberg lit her from above, emphasizing her brow and diminishing the size of her nose by this so-called "grace angle." In some close-ups, he positioned three "dinkies," or tiny spotlights, to meet just above her browline; with the help of a silver streak drawn in wax pencil down the bridge of her nose, these reduced its width. He had her hair dyed blonde. The rest of the vision was created by the camera lens. This was a custom-made lens called a "Rosher Bullseye" after the American photographer Charles Rosher, who had shot many Mary Pickford films. It replicated the human eye's impression of seeing only what it is looking at in sharp and detailed focus, while staying vaguely aware of related areas and objects. It clearly delineated Dietrich's main features, particularly the passionless glance of the female predator which Von Sternberg imposed on her, while allowing the rest of her face to recede into ever-so-soft focus. A remoteness is thus created: a disconcerting distance between Lola-Lola and ourselves that no focus-puller could measure, since it only exists in the spectator's erotic imagination. Lighting was making its psychological comment on the character: soon it would persuade us that we knew more about Dietrich than any information contained in the lines of dialogue.

She was now excited by all the attention she was getting. At the same time, she talked apprehensively of how the public might react to so raw a representation of a whore—a woman whose existence extracted the very essence of whoredom, rather than simply an errant human being with some redeeming qualities. In yet

"Dietrich seated on a barrel, lolling invitingly back in her cutaway skirt, her black suspenders tightly stretched against her pale legs, has become one of the best-known erotic icons in cinema history."

another mood, she would complain that she was not getting enough publicity for the important part she played.

Her "tormentor," familiar with the ways of overnight stardom in Hollywood, begged her to be patient. Her name would become much better known than anyone else's—at this stage, he neglected to add, "including mine." One has to ask, though, given the sensation that was in the making, why UFA did not exercise its contract option and retain Dietrich's services for subsequent films. Why give her the buildup only to have another studio gain the benefit? Incredibly, UFA allowed her to accept an offer of a Hollywood contract made by Paramount in mid-February 1930. She is said to have at first turned up her nose at the salary the Americans proposed, whereupon Von Sternberg gave her five minutes by his watch to make up her mind. "I have a faint recollection," he wrote sarcastically, "that the watch was torn from my grasp and flung away."

One of the reasons for UFA's neglecting to sign up Dietrich again was the public reaction they anticipated to a film, directed by an American, that made such a harsh mockery of German middle-class morality. Their apprehension was in fact groundless. Ironically, the attacks that came were from left-wing critics who accused the film of "selling out" Heinrich Mann's novel by *not* including the final, cynical chapter condemning the town's hypocrites. Right-wing critics, on the other hand, used the film as a stick to drub a novelist who had long been out of favor with the cinema and newspaper magnate Alfred Hugenberg. "In truth," wrote the influential Friedrich Hussong Neuland in *Der Montag Morgen* on the very eve of the première, "*The Blue Angel* is not a Heinrich Mann film—it is a film against him. Mann's book is the dirty, unsavory revenge of a truant schoolboy . . . his hero is a repulsive bag of malice. [But] the film is the story of a man who, from the first moment, has won our sympathy, a man lonely of spirit who is ruined with tragic consequences through his own weak character and, through inexperience, follows the false light which he takes to be a woman's love, but which is nothing but whoredom. Novel and film have nothing whatever in common. In one, we have a distorted view of an alleged social problem, in the other a true human fate."[19] This was a clever way of serving Hugenberg's profit while saving Hugenberg's face. Mann was driven to sending an angry telegram to the paper: "Suffice it to say that the film has been made with my cooperation and that the Professor Unrat role which Jannings has wished to play for a long time is my creation."

Von Sternberg alleges that even after they viewed the finished film, the UFA executives were not aware of the new star that had been made of Dietrich. But this is not quite the whole truth: with such a man, it seldom was. They had observed only too well how much one man's erotic fascination with Dietrich had contributed to the unmistakable success of the film's female lead. But they probably asked themselves, what would she be without this man to transform her? Von Sternberg showed no sign of wanting to stay on in Berlin. If UFA put Dietrich under contract, who would work with her, what properties would they have to offer her, and what could they themselves make of her? Lola-Lola was a striking creation, but not really repeatable. In words more familiar nowadays than then, her success was deemed to be a "one-off." If Dietrich wished to sign with Paramount, then let her—anyhow, UFA would still distribute the American films she made, supposing she was a success, back home in her native Germany. This is the way that a front-office mind functions in today's film industry: there is no reason to believe it was any more perceptive then.

Having assured herself that Von Sternberg would be her director in Hollywood, she agreed to Paramount's terms. Von Sternberg personally carried the contract back to Hollywood when he left Berlin some weeks before *The Blue Angel*'s première. This early departure is significant. His eye was already on his next film; he was investing something of his own power and success in using "his" star for personal aggrandizement in the city he knew to be impressed by such hubris, or, in its more commonplace Yiddish vernacular, *chutzpah*.

Mrs. von Sternberg later alleged that her husband's cold, haughty exterior concealed a fear that Dietrich would fail him. But his display of arrogant

Time for a glass of wine during a break in the production of *The Blue Angel*.

66

indifference was maintained right up to *The Blue Angel*'s première on April 1, 1930—"All Fools' Day," as he acidly noted in his memoirs. He did not return to Berlin for this fateful event. But he stage-managed things from afar, so that the première would no sooner have taken place than Dietrich would be on the high seas bound for America. Her ascension from earth to heaven could hardly have been better timed. A rehearsal of *The Blue Angel* was held at 1.00 a.m., on March 31, at UFA's showcase, the Gloria Palast cinema. Those present included Jannings, Pommer, Vollmöller, Zuckmayer, Erika and Klaus Mann (Heinrich's niece and nephew), but not Dietrich. On Von Sternberg's orders, she did not turn up until the second of the three screenings on April 1.

Peter Kreuder, the film's musical arranger, has preserved a highly charged memoir of that occasion which attests to the furious tensions present in the reception room whose glass-windowed front overlooked the main auditorium. Jannings was in a towering rage. He had found out at the last minute that Von Sternberg had ordered Kreuder to have a theatrical "blackout" inserted in the film just after the song "Falling in Love Again," in order to cue the audience's applause for Dietrich. The two men came to blows upon Kreuder's refusal to remove it. Jannings, his back often turned to the screen, kept up a sarcastic exchange with his cronies, while Dietrich, escorted by Willi Forst, pressed her nose excitedly against the window as the audience's mounting approval filtered through to her.

When it was all over, the audience was on its feet acclaiming a new star, whose name was not Jannings. "Marlene . . . Marlene" rose the cries that critics were quick to articulate in print. "One is virtually stunned by Fräulein Dietrich's performance," wrote one tradepaper reviewer. The critic Herbert Ihering of the *Berliner Börsen-Courier* wrote: "The film's revelation"—an often repeated word—"is Marlene Dietrich. She sings and acts almost without show of emotion"—another frequent comment—"but this calculated phlegmatism is provocative. She is vulgar without seeming to act. Everything in the film is cinema, not theater."[20] Even a critic not usually well disposed to Dietrich, Wolf Zucker in *Die literarische Welt*, conceded, "Astounding what has been made of Marlene Dietrich, an actress one did not always watch with pleasure in earlier films. This time she succeeds in everything . . . even singing."[21]

Yet it would be untrue to assert (as has sometimes been done) that Dietrich eclipsed Jannings. She did not. Except for a few critics who were overfamiliar with Jannings's ponderously self-abasing style, most of the press praised "the depth of his acting," its "almost unbelievable reality" and its "intensity and conviction almost never before attained by stage actors in the films." Yet even his admirers, like Hans Sahl in *Der Montag Morgen*, ended up avowing: "The revelation of the film is neither Sternberg nor Jannings: it is Marlene Dietrich. . . . This is no longer a fake Garbo. Everything about her is novel and exciting. Her alluring and enticing walk, her dispassionate decadence, her sensual aggressiveness in the way she speaks and moves. Marlene Dietrich has left for

Von Sternberg and Dietrich, Berlin 1929—"an artistic opportunity to create in the flesh the woman he fantasized in his mind."

68

Hollywood. The German cinema is poorer by an artist."[22] It was quite a journey, to have come from the ranks of the extra girls and, within five years, to be departing one's homeland with such plaudits ringing in the ears.

Again we are fortunate in having a witness to this moment in her life. Stefan Lorant, who had done that cruel and abortive screen test on the naive and bedazzled girl some six years earlier, happened to run into Dietrich in between screenings on the day of *The Blue Angel*'s première. She was having dinner with a friend at the Eden Hotel, "looking sad and forlorn." "'Aren't you happy even yet, after what you have just accomplished?' I asked her. She did not reply, but only looked at me, very, very sadly. I suppose she was thinking of the years of struggle, of all the privations, misery and want. Even now she could not be happy. It all seemed too unreal. She did not dare rejoice yet."[23]

She took her bow before a vociferous audience at the third and last performance of her film that evening, then made a hasty, hopefully unobserved exit from the back of the theater and, still in her ermine wrap and champagne-hued gown, was hoisted bodily aboard a tarpaulin-covered truck already loaded with forty pieces of traveling luggage. It inched its way through the heavy traffic, then accelerated towards the Lehrter Bahnhof in order to catch the 11.00 p.m. boat train to Bremerhaven, from where the great liner *Bremen* was to sail that night for New York. As Kreuder recalls it, he and an ebullient Willi Forst sat with Dietrich on the jolting luggage or thumped out the *Blue Angel* melodies on an upright piano. More champagne was opened, the mood grew crazy, and as the big truck bumped and swayed down the cobbled streets the exuberant trio drank to the future and, says Kreuder, tossed their empty glasses out into the night.

UFA had forewarned the railroad officials, and the train waited just long enough to see Dietrich aboard. Then, like an exotic *femme fatale* from some Von Sternberg fantasy, she stood alone at the window and raised her presentation bouquet of roses, lilac and lilies like a valediction to the city, the friends, the home, the child and the husband she had been induced to quit for the uncertain promises of Hollywood.

HOLLYWOOD

HOLLYWOOD

On subsequent transatlantic voyages, Dietrich was to keep a calculated distance between herself and other passengers unless they too were celebrities or she had earlier made their acquaintance. This is not to be wondered at: it is the commonplace protectiveness of those who have already found fame or fortune and wish to be spared the curiosity or importunities of those who have not. But on this voyage, Dietrich herself had as yet no fortune and only restricted fame—and the latter was bound to recede the farther the liner sailed from Germany. She was also very, very lonely. Hence she welcomed the attention paid her by two "ordinary Americans." Not quite ordinary, perhaps, since Jimmy and Bianca Brooks at least possessed important film-industry and theatrical links. Brooks's costume emporium clothed the stars; his wife was a costume designer; and their daughter Geraldine Brooks was to become a notable stage and screen actress in the next decade. Budd Schulberg, son of the then production boss at Paramount, whose parent company, Famous Players-Lasky, had just hired Dietrich, later married Geraldine, and, through his in-laws, was able to include in his memoirs an intriguing vignette of those days at sea aboard the *Bremen.*

Schulberg recalls how the actress was much attracted to Jimmy Brooks because of his New York-style wit, which had the flavor of Berlin's street-wise mockery. She spent so much time in his company, according to Schulberg, that Mrs. Brooks had to be sent a penitential bouquet of flowers every day of the voyage. Dietrich fascinated Mrs. Brooks, too, with the worldliness of her approach to things that were still generally only mentioned in undertones. Mrs. Brooks was rather surprised by an album of camera studies of females, some of whom were embracing each other. Quite commonplace in Berlin, Dietrich assured her. This indeed was a liberated woman talking, Mrs. Brooks decided. They kept up their acquaintance after they disembarked and went their separate ways. It was to Brooks's that Dietrich later turned to rent the man's dress suit which she sported, with white tie and cane, on her nightclub outings in New York in the 1930s. A good advertisement for all parties; and, as Dietrich herself used to point out, men's wear came more cheaply than women's gowns: Teutonic practicality was never far from her thoughts, however much her extravagant appearance contradicted it. Brooks, too, made up some of the fabulously embroidered clothes she was to wear in her postwar concert performances.

Portrait by Irving Chidnoff, photographed soon after Dietrich's arrival in New York, April 1930.

72

Before boarding the Los Angeles-bound train in Chicago, the newly arrived star from Germany obligingly posed for newspaper photographers atop her luggage, with one arm resting on her violin case. Dietrich's destination was the Paramount Studios in Hollywood, identified on this contemporary photo as "the gateway of the famous and portal to riches for many an unknown."

But her arrival in New York on April 9, 1930, was not nearly so agreeable as that shipboard encounter. She was put through the pierside ritual (which all European film artists, even the divine Garbo, were obliged to suffer) of the hucstering directness of news photographers—aided and abetted, it must be admitted, by studio publicists. Dietrich perched atop her luggage and showed her legs to America. Worse followed at the press conference at the Ritz-Carlton. Von Sternberg flew into a rage when he heard this had been arranged; for from the minute she arrived in Hollywood, he personally was to handle or approve *all* contact with the media. He knew how to protect a star as well as build one; and Dietrich needed protection quite as much as exposure at this stage. Since no one in the New York press corps had seen even a foot of her films, or knew what she was to do in America, she was quizzed insensitively on the "human interest" of being a "Hollywood discovery" and asked why she was not accompanied by her husband. Even worse from Paramount's point of view, she was sternly interrogated about why she had left behind in Germany her daughter of tender years.

Still, shaken by this encounter with people whom she would ever afterwards view as only a little friendlier and more trustworthy than a time bomb, Dietrich was rushed before the camera of Irving Chidnoff, a notable portraitist, whose studio photographs illuminate clearly enough the wonderfully sculptured flesh and bone that Von Sternberg was soon to paint even more alluringly with his own particular light and shade. There was good reason for taking pictures in New York rather than waiting for her arrival in Hollywood. These studies destined for the smart glossy magazines of New York were akin to a calling card. They made the new acquisition "accepted" in the way a set of studio stills didn't. Sometimes they even alerted the studios, 3,000 miles distant, to what they had "bought blind" when they went shopping for talent in Europe. Just such a a set of photographs of the little-known Greta Garbo, published in *Vanity Fair* in 1925, showed her unique but rarely revealed physical beauty so well that the very studio which had engaged her, Metro-Goldwyn-Mayer, became excited enough actually to use her.

Comparisons between Dietrich and Garbo were inevitable: there is evidence that Paramount even welcomed them. Films are not basically a creative art: they are an imitative industry. What is most often imitated is someone else's proven success. Dietrich arrived in Hollywood towards the end of April 1930 and made her first public appearance—"public" in the sense of being shown off to the film community—at a reception given by the family of B. P. Schulberg (her boss, that is) at the Beverly Wilshire Hotel. It was not a party for Dietrich: it was a prelude to the wedding of Louis B. Mayer's daughter Irene to the newly fledged producer David O. Selznick. Present in strength were MGM's top men, Mayer, Thalberg, J. Robert Rubin, Harry Rapf and others. It was like Paramount's idea of serving notice on "Garbo's studio" of the rival outfit's stellar challenger. "Midway in the evening," Irene Mayer Selznick has recalled, "there was a sudden hush, as though a cue had been given. Marlene Dietrich, fresh from her triumph in *The Blue Angel*, made a spectacular entrance, followed by Josef von Sternberg. She strode across the full length of the enormous dance floor. The silence was broken by applause. She had arrived in Hollywood that day, and her debut caused such a flurry she practically seemed guest of honor."[24]

Like Garbo, too, the transplanted Dietrich at first hated Hollywood—everything about it. It was a company town, not a capital city. Its rigid work demarcations did duty for the social strata of Europe. It lacked Berlin's churning conviviality and the zestful vulgarity, never mind the easy sexual tolerances, of its café life.

There was nowhere to go: at least, nowhere that Dietrich cared to go, for Von Sternberg arranged their social engagements quite as much as their work schedule and he despised the "Coconut Grove Culture," as he called it, preferring the company of books and magazines imported from Europe. "At first he allowed no direct contact with Dietrich, none at all," says Sam Jaffe, a Paramount executive at the time, later an agent, and not to be confused with that other Sam Jaffe, the actor (and Dietrich's co-star in *The Scarlet Empress*).[25] According to Jaffe:

He was her representative, her agent, her chaperone. In all my days at Paramount, I never saw a man who took a piece of clay and so ruthlessly shaped it to his will as Von Sternberg did with Dietrich. He gave direction to her career as well as definition to her image: no other director on the lot did that.

Von Sternberg had sent over the tests he had made of Dietrich in Berlin, walking, sitting down, turning her head this way and that, singing a bit. She looked fascinating: moreover, she was not expensive to hire. So what had Paramount to lose by putting her under contract? She would be a European name for a European market, which at that time was important.

It was calculated that foreign territories then accounted for sixty percent of a film's revenues. Jaffe continues:

You could not think of Dietrich without Von Sternberg. She was at first the house guest of Josef and his wife. Generally they did not go out much. They liked being alone together. They closed the door and were not at home to anyone. The studio tolerated such a relationship because, after all, if it was good for their pictures the studio would make a lot of money: if it wasn't, they'd go their own, separate ways soon enough anyhow.

Paramount was a more "European" studio than any of its Hollywood peers: not in the sense of possessing a large complement of first-generation Americans, for Universal and MGM were also well blessed with Central and East European sons, but in the rather more sophisticated view it took of certain kinds of human relationships which—over at MGM, say—would have caused Mayer to perform one of his famous fainting fits of indignation. The Dietrich-Von Sternberg duo was "par" for Paramount, so to speak. In any case, as Jaffe says:

Contrary to the usual gossip about personal relationships that one heard at the studio, it was believed by most people that Von Sternberg did *not* sleep with her, and I tend to believe it. I don't think Dietrich found him physically very appealing. She had far more character than he had, she showed more principle than he did. For example, she was to

Prior to starting work on her first Hollywood film, Dietrich embarked on a rigorous routine of dieting, exercise and cosmetic treatment. The results are apparent in this portrait by E. R. Richee, made in mid-1930.

With a photo of her
daughter propped on the
bedside table, Dietrich places
a transatlantic telephone call
to her Berlin home for the
benefit of Erich Salomon's
camera. The inset portrait is
again by E. R. Richee.

adopt an attitude of scorn and ostracism towards Hitler right from the start that Von Sternberg never took at all, despite his being Jewish. He was the total artist, but quite apolitical. I think he would have liked them to have a closer relationship of the physical kind: he was quite broken up later on when she struck out independently, though he put on his usual pose of arrogant indifference.

On the other hand, he definitely had something this woman needed.

Von Sternberg made Dietrich submit to disciplined dieting and exercise designed to bring her figure into line with his fantasy. She was given the studio's cosmetic treatment that made her too, too solid Berlin flesh literally melt. Her eyebrows were shaved to the shape of those familiar flyaway antennae, though it was rigorous abstinence which induced her cheek hollows, not teeth-pulling, the rumor of which in later days used to send her into a paroxysm of caustic laughter as she listed the celebrities who had had their teeth "done" to assist their looks. As far as report can be relied on, all Dietrich's teeth stayed hers. Massage slimmed her lower limbs to even svelter proportions, her ankles being sometimes bandaged so as to disperse the slightest tendency to fat at this crucial juncture. It was said that her fondness for wearing trousers owed something to the need to conceal these surgical bindings. But she always maintained that pants were simply more comfortable, and, amid other sartorial *exotica* to be seen in Hollywood, they didn't cause the raised eyebrows that shot up in more conventional social circles. What is often forgotten is that Dietrich's display of trousers in public was often sensational simply because of the formal setting (lunches, dinner parties, etc.) in which she wore them.

Her early unhappiness in Hollywood probably assisted her fleshly mortification. She cried, literally, for the daughter she had left behind. Not even the gramophone recordings filled with "baby talk" and other intimacies, which she made to send back to Berlin, would bring nearer the five-year-old Heidede. Work was probably a comfort to her: in the studio she could have no thought for anyone but the martinet who was drilling her.

She is said to have been shocked when her mentor proposed a story called *Amy Jolly, The Woman of Marrakesh* as their first Hollywood film. Maybe she was: she had given him the novel (written by a Berlin journalist, Benno Vigny, and reputed to be based on his early life in the French Foreign Legion) simply in order to help Von Sternberg pass the time on the journey back to America from Berlin. But Paramount had already acquired rights in the book before Von Sternberg stowed it away in his cabin luggage: Jules Furthman, a contract writer, had been working on a screen treatment even before the director arrived back on the welcome mat. The need for speed in presenting an "American" Dietrich to the public on the screen was intensified because *The Blue Angel* was being deliberately held back from the American market until its star had been publicized and made known. Talkie techniques were becoming monthly more sophisticated, and a film made in Germany earlier in the year could literally sound very *passé* if it remained on the shelf too long.

Amy Jolly was soon renamed *Morocco* because its star, Gary Cooper, didn't take kindly to a German import like Dietrich acquiring the eponymous importance conferred by the original title. The crucial task was to remake the image of Dietrich psychologically as well as physically, so that she would appeal to the Main Street American: in short, she had to be humanized and rendered capable of returning a man's love, maybe at some sacrifice to herself, instead of destroying him as the demonic Lola-Lola had been wont to do. Cooper wasn't a "moth" to be consumed by anyone's "flame," since Hollywood mythology decreed that stars must not suffer sexual degradation: they must not play weak or perpetually blemished characters beyond redemption by their own strength of will or by the flattering love that a woman may lavish on their convalescent souls.

So *Morocco* was made palatable to American filmgoers by letting Legionnaire Tom Brown (Cooper) coolly receive Amy's tokens of love, but leave this foreign heartbreaker in the lurch at the end. The movie fades out on a scene that is notorious in the annals of "camp cinema," with a vision of Dietrich in an evening gown shedding her cocotte's life-style as well as her high heels and walking off through the Moorish town gateway in the company of less fashion-conscious "women of the desert," her heart and steps directed gamely (but, one fears, soon lamely) towards the disappearing Legion and her lover.

By thus causing *her*, rather than the man, to be "humiliated," by bringing her down to the same level as other vulnerable mortals, the story reversed the "European" resolution of *The Blue Angel* and this time encouraged Dietrich to show her feelings.

Yet its structure is canny enough to leave room for that element of perversity which Europeans would feel gratified at seeing, and Americans (of that era) excitingly shocked. Thus, clad in white tie, top hat and tails (not, it must be said, a costume naturally chosen for wear, even by cabaret singers, in those hot latitudes), she sings the ambiguously titled "What Am I Bid for My Apples?" to the macho men of the Legion and expatriate sophisticates in the place's principal café, and plants a kiss on the lips of an attractively startled young girl: a touch of homophile affection just about permissible at that time in Hollywood before the refurbished Production Code (and the sharper dragon's teeth of the Roman Catholic Legion of Decency, which was to be formed three years later) forced the studios into more hypocritical subtleties of titillation. But these sexual tricks apart, what stamped Dietrich on to filmgoers' imaginations was the way she was presented visually on the screen. Von Sternberg wrapped her in more metaphysical material than men's suiting.

Lee Garmes, *Morocco*'s lighting photographer, later laid claim to creating the classic Dietrich image. He says he at first followed the director's instruction to light her from one side only: but then the daily "rushes" showed him that what this was producing was a second Garbo. Whereupon, without telling Von Sternberg, Garmes reverted to the "north" lighting he himself preferred. This brought out Dietrich's cheekbones and created a fascinating dissonance between

A scene from *Morocco*, Dietrich's first American film, with Gary Cooper as the Legionnaire who remains in the end impervious to temptation. The portrait reproduced on page 77 can be seen here tacked to the wall. From Berlin the actress had brought a collection of good-luck talismans, including a black golliwog and a Japanese doll (*inset*). She insinuated them into the set dressing of her films wherever she could, as in the right foreground of the above scene from *Morocco*.

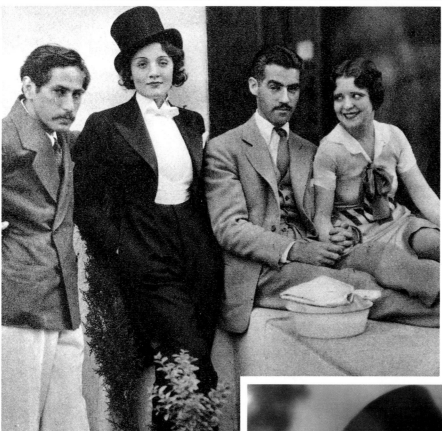

Morocco afforded Von Sternberg his first opportunity to put Dietrich in full male attire. A photo taken on the Paramount lot (*above*) catches him, Dietrich, director Frank Tuttle and Clara Bow off duty, while the studio still (*right*) shows the star as she appeared in the film.

Opposite: Dietrich and Cooper pose on set for lighting cameraman Lee Garmes. The still (*inset*) shows Adolphe Menjou as the debonair dilettante who hopes to buy Dietrich's favors.

her heavy eyelids and the playfulness of those artificial eyebrows penciled in an inch above them.

The simple truth is that each man's expertise and vision probably modified the other's. A director who knew nothing about lighting—and Hollywood had (and has) plenty such—would not have contested Garmes's claim: he would probably not have been aware of it as such—the guy was simply being paid to do his job, which was "light." But Von Sternberg, besides being a visionary, was also a practical and most proficient lighting photographer—only craft-union rules prevented his taking the credit for lighting until he at last got his card and put his name on *The Devil Is a Woman*. However, the way Garmes made Dietrich look on the screen was probably near enough to the way Von Sternberg saw her in his mind's eye: only minor adjustments were necessary, since each man saw essentially the same Dietrich.

It was Von Sternberg, though, who fused himself emotionally and spiritually with what he saw. As he once told Peter Bogdanovich, "I am Miss Dietrich—Miss Dietrich is *me*." Dietrich confirmed this when Bogdanovich asked her if the remark upset her. "No—because it was true." From *Morocco* on, everything in a Von Sternberg-Dietrich film—lenses, lighting, shadows and the veiling of a dozen different substances and textures from lace to mist, smoke and steam—creates its own psychological comment on player and character. No secret ever came as well wrapped up as Marlene Dietrich. André Malraux once compared her to "a myth like Phryne," rather than to an actress like Bernhardt. One can see what he meant, but the comparison happens to be singularly inapposite. Phryne was the notorious Athenian courtesan of the fourth century BC who tried to discompose the judges in the act of sentencing her by stripping off her clothes. This was hardly Dietrich's style. Had Von Sternberg been defending Phryne, he would never have let her appear in court other than fully clad from the neck down, and maybe he would have added a half-veil or, quite possibly, put her in breeches. *Morocco* served notice that, where Dietrich's eroticism was concerned, her director was the great coverer-up.

But lighting was only part of the secret of his presentation of her. He "edited" her whole personality, starting with the way she spoke. Although she knew English, she did not yet know it confidently enough to handle long sentences—even an unusual word threw her. This is one reason for Von Sternberg's notching up such an abnormal number of takes in filming the scenes. Her intonation must fit her mysterious *persona*: hence the stylized tone he developed for both. He had an even more practical and urgent reason: he knew that Paramount's front office had signed up the star on *his* assurance that she would make good (and he would make her better) in Hollywood. He could not risk any dissatisfaction when Adolph Zukor and B. P. Schulberg viewed the daily rushes. The ones he ordered to be printed out of the dozens he shot were those where Dietrich was perfect in word, deed and looks. Shooting was like a war of attrition until everything came out right. Indeed he found that pushing her harder and harder, forcing the issue to the fiftieth take or more, seemed to make his leading lady even more desirous of pleasing him.

"I remember in *Morocco*, I had a scene with Cooper," she told Bogdanovich in 1973, "I was supposed to go to the door, turn and say a line like, 'Wait for me,' and then leave. And Von Sternberg said, 'Walk to the door, count to ten, say your line and leave.' So I did and he got very angry. 'If you're so stupid that you can't count slowly, then count to twenty-five.' And we did it again. I think we did it forty times, until finally I was counting probably to fifty. And I didn't know why." Dietrich was annoyed, but formidable compensation was to hand. "At the première of *Morocco* . . . when this moment came and I paused and then said, 'Wait for me,' the audience burst into applause. Von Sternberg knew they were waiting for this—and he made them wait, and they loved it."[26] But a penalty had to be paid, too. "My reputation as one of the swiftest directors in films was dealt quite a blow," Von Sternberg admitted.

The temperaments as well as the skills of both the star and her director were doing something else to Dietrich besides creating an erotic illusion of her in people's minds. The Dietrich image was being formed through a romantic association with certain kinds of men and certain codes of behavior. In both cases, they were military. Her lover's first allegiance in *Morocco* is not to his woman, but to his regiment; and Dietrich, too, has to "join up," become one of "the legion of lost women" before she stands a chance of getting him (supposing she survives the desert trek). She answers the regiment's call, passing up the life of civilian leisure and comfort offered by Adolphe Menjou's wealthy dilettante. The warrior virtues of a life shared with fighting men were henceforth a constant factor in all but one of the movies Dietrich made with Von Sternberg. It shapes her relationships with the male stars; it gives her a comradeship with the characters they play; it predates their love together and sometimes survives it.

Even though the male attire she wears in *Morocco* does not come from a military tailor—not yet, though it soon would—it is a sort of sexual *uniform* that she is issued with when she enlists in her own particular company of women. It represents her attitude to life, just as the soldier's uniform represents *his* profession; and she, too, carries the badges of rank. Soldiers in Dietrich films are forever saluting her, not just out of courtesy, but in recognition of the fact that both of them belong to the same way of life if not the same sex. Her character's lesbian affection for the young girl in the Arab café in *Morocco* is a sort of masonic hint that though they do not share the same profession their inclinations are nevertheless in harmony. Once it is perceived or sensed that these things create a certain feeling about a star, they are quickly absorbed by screenwriters into what becomes the star's dominant public image. With the backing of her autocratic director, Dietrich's image was to be one that her father and stepfather would have recognized and saluted inside or outside their barrack gates.

Von Sternberg did not like directing Gary Cooper. The star was so tall: the director so small. Therefore Dietrich was posed above him as often as possible, in

order to make Cooper look up at her. Dietrich enabled Von Sternberg to *impose* himself on male actors—a breed he detested—and at the same time assuage the jealousy arising from what he sensed were his own romantic deficiencies. One can well imagine the eddies and undercurrents on the closed set.

Almost as soon as *Morocco* finished shooting, Dietrich was rushed into her second American film. Her code name "X-27" was the original title of this World War I espionage melodrama in which she played a Mata Hari-like spy. But Paramount insisted the title be changed and it became *Dishonored*, though Von Sternberg sarcastically noted that any lady who wound up before a firing squad was likely to be dead long before she could be dishonored. He wrote the story himself: a throwaway excuse for filtering Dietrich's sex appeal through the conflicting loyalties of war. Now the great, warm, comforting Lili Marlene-like figure of the prostitute who plies her trade in the streets is allied to the woman who lives (and dies) by a different code of honor. Her opening remark, which persuades the passing spymaster to recruit her, is: "I'm not afraid of life, though I'm not afraid of death, either." It sounds like a free translation of a regimental motto.

Dietrich is cast as an officer's widow who has taken to prostitution out of economic necessity; but one feels that her heart is in the trade, too, the minute one hears her coo of "Helloo" directed at the chief of the Austrian Secret Service. "I need a woman who knows how to deal with men," he tells her—and her eyes smile cynically at this euphemism. Everything about the film is interpreted in military terms that give Dietrich's performance a rivetingly masculine resonance. Her entrance into the Secret Service headquarters is like that of a visiting general: a physical thrill passes through the roomful of uniformed men. It's almost as if they expect mobilization to be imminent. Later on, when she traps her first traitor (a Von Sternberg figure who surrenders his sword to her—an irony one hopes both star and director appreciated) he murmurs just before shooting himself, "What a charming evening we might have had, if you had not been a spy and I a traitor." "Then," she reminds him, "we might never have met." One can say the same thing, *mutatis mutandis*, about Von Sternberg and Dietrich: *Dishonored*'s element of autobiography makes one feel one is eavesdropping on a cynical coded conversation between them carried out in the guise of the film dialogue.

But if Dietrich's love is military in style, it is by no means patriotic in direction. She is a patriot for the heart rather than for any particular nation. *Dishonored* helped Dietrich establish her international appeal as a woman without territorial allegiances—someone whom no single passport is wide enough to encompass. Lili Marlene, after all, was a front-line folk heroine who, according to whichever lips hummed her tale, could move from one battle line to the other without forfeiting any loyalties or betraying any lover. Dietrich came to be seen this way, too. Much, much later she was to tell an interviewer, "Ever since I lost my country and my language, ever since I left Germany in 1930, I've been a traveler without any roots."

The classic "fade out" scene from *Morocco*, as Dietrich in bare feet and swirling skirt sets out across the Sahara towards the disappearing Legion. Inside the town walls, a group of the film's Legionnaires, along with director Von Sternberg, Gary Cooper and two camels, take time off to pose for a publicity photograph (*inset, right*).

At the end of *Dishonored*, she alludes to the idea of uniform and the freemasonry of the street sorority which constitutes her own "army." "Can you help me die in a uniform of my own choosing?" she asks the priest, when she is about to go to her execution. "Any dress I was wearing when I served my countrymen, not my country." Understanding man of God!—he brings her her old streetwalker's clothes. She pauses with superb effrontery to make her face up in the gleaming blade of an officer's ceremonial sword: even her toilette has warlike accouterments. Then she walks "professionally" out to face the firing squad, gratefully utilizing the brief respite when the officer in charge breaks down in tears to touch up her lipstick and straighten the seam of her stocking. Such a scene is absurd in the recollection or the telling. But as Von Sternberg films it, it works like a *coup de théâtre*: Dietrich is so plainly treating her execution as if it were an assignation. It is as if she is going to meet not her maker, but her lover.

Dying a soldier's death by the soldiers' hands: it is the scene that wins Dietrich her commission—promotion into the company of fighting men which was to preoccupy her, off and on, in films and in life, until the wartime years allowed her to achieve the reality of it. Von Sternberg plucked the martial chord: but Dietrich kept it vibrating.

Flash forward precisely thirty years from the date of *Dishonored* to Stanley Kramer's production of *Judgment at Nuremberg* in 1961, in which she played the widow of another general—only this time it is her husband who has been executed, for war crimes. By now, Dietrich's own feelings about Hitler and the German people were well known. She blamed them both for the war. It was assumed that she had accepted the role in order to bring the guilt home to the generation that stayed in Germany, supported Hitler, and so made his war possible. No doubt this played its part in her thinking. But the character of Frau Bertholt, as she appears in Abby Mann's screenplay, corresponds more closely to a *pre-Hitler* Dietrich. She is a woman whose love for her husband excuses everything. She cannot believe him guilty of war crimes. Above all, she cannot accept the manner in which he was put to death. This outrages her own devotion to military ideals and a soldier's dignity. "He was entitled to a soldier's death," she keeps insisting. "He asked for that. I tried to get that for him . . . just that he be permitted the dignity of a firing squad. You know what happened. He was hanged with the others." "Dishonor" there might be, but, in her book, the manner of one's dying expunges it.

Morocco was released in America on November 16, 1930; *The Blue Angel*, on December 5, 1930; *Dishonored*, on March 6, 1931. This succession of virtually back-to-back releases, along with the enormous combined advertising budget (said to be over a half million dollars) that Paramount put behind them, made it seem as if Dietrich had suddenly come out of nowhere, fully established as a star. American filmgoers got no chance to familiarize themselves with her slow ascent from bit-parts to leading roles in her seventeen earlier movies. At a stroke, there she was.

Another portrait by E. R. Richee from 1930.

88

In *Dishonored*, Dietrich's second American film, she plays the part of a spy code-named X-27. In the Secret Service headquarters (*above*), "a physical thrill passes through the roomful of uniformed men" when she enters. Her costumes in the film run the gamut from an aviatrix's leather cover-all to a *femme fatale*'s sequined cape and tunic. On location to shoot an outdoor scene, Von Sternberg obliged a Paramount publicist by posing with a local state trooper (*inset*).

One finds the American press referring to her, until quite late in the 1930s, as "a German actress" or "the German star," and she undoubtedly added a new flavor of exoticism to American cinema. The only person on record as not having heard of her in 1931, according to one motion-picture poll, was Greta Garbo. ("Who is Marlene Dietrich?" she reportedly replied.) Richard Watts, Jr., reviewing *Dishonored*, said: "Miss Dietrich . . . proves once more that her hasty [*sic*] rise to film celebrity was the result of neither luck, accident nor publicity. There still may be some doubt whether she possesses that technical expertise on which so many observers place such store, but there can be little question by now that her almost lyrically ironic air of detachment and, to be as frank about it as possible, her physical appeal make her one of the great personages." To use "great" about an actress after only two American films is surely a very rare event in critical practice.

Dietrich left for Europe in December 1930 immediately *Dishonored* finished shooting. She had been so homesick from the start that Paramount felt morally obliged to revise her contract, changing it from the standard seven-year term with options to a two-picture deal. Her salary went up—from $75,000 to $125,000 a picture. On her return to America, in April 1931, she was accompanied by her daughter. Heidede was then six: Dietrich may have been upset by reports from Sieber of how much she was missing her mother. Her father, too, was living his own life, with much of his wife's independence. Sieber had taken up with a woman strongly resembling Dietrich in looks, a Russian-born actress-singer, whom he lived with and maintained for much of his life without alienating his wife's affections.

Indeed, Dietrich seems to have been very understanding about the situation. And why not? It may have appealed to her practical nature. It gave her the advantage of being a married woman and thus having a cast-iron excuse for avoiding binding proposals that her men friends might make in response to her obvious enjoyment of their company. At the same time she was not encumbered in selecting her companions by the physical presence of a husband. To many members of the public, in fact, she seemed a free woman. Sieber faded into the European scene, where he became a minor employee of Paramount in Berlin and later Paris, responsible for dubbing films (including his wife's). After World War II, he took up chicken farming in California's San Fernando Valley. A sign saying "EGGS," with two cowbells attached inviting passers-by to ring for service, hardly suggested associations with the exotic Dietrich. Her "silent partner" abided by her wishes and, on the very few occasions when he responded to a reporter shaking the cowbells, he sounded like a man reading the subtitles on a foreign film: "The bond between us is just as strong as ever. Only death will end our marriage." (And, in fact, only death did.)

But if Dietrich was thus able to avoid affronting convention by her reported liaisons with male celebrities, she did not avoid one totally unjustified but embarrassing public attack on her when she returned to New York from Europe

Dietrich left for Europe as soon as *Dishonored* finished shooting. Before her train pulled out of the Los Angeles station she was photographed in her Pullman compartment, garbed in mannish attire and clutching some of her newly-earned American dollars. She went on to Berlin to visit her husband, Rudolf Sieber (*above, right*). By April 1931, Dietrich had returned to Hollywood with her daughter, Heidede, and shortly thereafter they were joined by Sieber. Just to show it was a truly happy family, and to quell any incipient scandal-mongering, a Paramount photographer posed the three Siebers in company with Josef von Sternberg (*below*).

in 1931. She was met at the pier and served with two writs. Both were from Riza Royce von Sternberg: one alleged that Dietrich had stolen her husband's love, and claimed damages of $500,000; the other sued for a libel alleged to have been uttered by Dietrich and published in a Viennese periodical. Confusion persists to this day—due to the parties' discretion at the time—over Von Sternberg's exact relationship with his then wife. He is usually said to have been married to her twice, the second time following a divorce at the end of the 1920s; but there are grounds for believing that the first divorce was not valid under California law and the remarriage that followed took place simply to regulate things for a second and final divorce in the 1930s. Whatever the truth of this, Paramount took Mrs. von Sternberg's writs seriously enough to soothe the offended lady into silence. And a persistent Dietrich wrung an admission from the Viennese journalist concerned that he had made up the remark about Mrs. von Sternberg attributed to the star.

At any rate, the *petit scandale* had the effect of bringing Rudi Sieber post-haste to California so as to be with his wife and child and to show the world a united family front of affection, devotion and convention. The press followed his journey to Marlene from the moment he arrived in New York (saying such homely things as "She will fix me my dish of *Eierkuchen* [omelet] as soon as I get there" and registering surprise that his wife was not yet famous in America for her culinary ability) to the moment he stepped off the Santa Fe Chief at Pasadena to be embraced so soundly by his wife that it was a long time (according to waiting newsmen clocking the seconds) "before he could place his right hand under his wife's chin and give her one dutiful peck." The "united family" effect was scarcely impaired by the presence of Josef von Sternberg "attired in white topped off by a black beret" sitting in the rear of the car which brought Marlene and Heidede (sitting up front with the chauffeur) to the station.

Marlene, as reported by the fashion correspondent who had been tipped off about the arrival so that the press might record more than the simple documentary details about marital conventions being observed, was described as wearing "a sports costume consisting of a white felt hat, white blouse, light tan mohair skirt, sheer tan hose, white and tan Oxfords, and a russet four-in-hand peppered with white dots." The correspondent added, slightly waspishly, that "little Maria" (as Heidede had become known on arrival in America) wore a "pink and filmy" frock that was "all feminine, lacking the boyish note of that worn by her rival [for Sieber's affections]." The report concluded: "The family trio entered the car—this time Von Sternberg sitting up front with the chauffeur—[and] as the machine started for Beverly Hills, the 'languid queen of the Kleig lights' placed both arms about Rudi and whispered softly."

This well-publicized cameo of motherhood supported one convention, yet ironically contributed to shattering another. Hollywood stars at that time, 1931, knew the advantages of advertising their sex appeal by frequent marriages, yet they still shied away from what such a union usually produced in the case of plainer folk, namely children. Hollywood feared that for an actress motherhood

A 1931 photo by E. R. Richee of Dietrich and daughter (now renamed Maria) served to underline the star's "proud and public display of very European-style affection for her child."

was incompatible with stardom: fans, it was believed, would desert a star if they saw her in the image of a parent. But Dietrich's proud and public display of very European-style affection for her child actually began to increase her fan mail. The idea swiftly caught on in Beverly Hills. Soon Norma Shearer was posing with her one-year-old son by Irving Thalberg; the offspring of Bebe Daniels and Ben Lyon was being photographed almost as often as its parents; and other stars who had never thought of having babies shrewdly concluded that they, too, would have the eyes of the world—or, at least, that part of it covered by the Hollywood press corps—focused on them for the better part of twelve months if they announced they were "expecting."

Von Sternberg got back to work as soon as Rudi Sieber had returned to Paris; and he made what many critics regard as his finest film with Dietrich: *Shanghai Express.* "Few of his films," wrote John Baxter, "are so tightly integrated in decor and performance as this brilliant visual improvisation on the chosen location, China, the chosen subject, as usual deception and desire, and the chosen focus for this confrontation, the blinding white carriages of the Shanghai Express."[27] (In fact, it was a train on loan from the Santa Fe Railroad, repainted gleaming white with Chinese calligraphy decorating its sides.) "Von Sternberg," says Sam Jaffe, "was very acute in picking the right backgrounds for his Dietrich stories—faraway places, or distant periods of history, always with a touch, or more than a touch, of exoticism about them. The only film he made with her which didn't fit these requirements, the contemporary American scene in *Blonde Venus*, turned out to be their least successful Hollywood film: the background was anti-Dietrich."

The story of a group of travelers held hostage by a Chinese warlord takes place almost entirely aboard the train as it thunders along from Peking to Shanghai, light and shade alternating in its corridors and compartments and the endless Chinese symbols underlining the moral ambiguities of countryside and travelers. It is evocative, however unhistorical; erotic, however cliché-ridden; decorative, however ersatz. Von Sternberg sarcastically called it "a picture of a train, not a picture of Marlene." But Dietrich stalks on to the platform at the start, striking the film's black-and-white keynote in her black feather boa and an eye veil that makes the visible lower half of her haughtily mysterious face look as if it is plastered with cold cream, it is so vividly white by contrast.

This creature of the half-light and the *demi-monde* is Shanghai Lily, and the chiaroscuro she constantly moves in establishes that her goodness is only half obscured by her worldliness. When she says to Clive Brook, as the army officer sharing the perils of the journey, "Once upon a time we loved each other," something more useful than this trite line floats out of her mouth—namely a cloud of cigarette smoke, wreathing round her face like the physical manifestation of smoldering reminiscence.

Von Sternberg was now very sure of what John Baxter calls these "significant minutiae" in his mood-movies. Sometimes he "sectionalizes" Dietrich, letting a

Shanghai Express is generally held to be Von Sternberg's finest film with Dietrich. An early scene shows the tantalizing Shanghai Lily in her compartment, along with Anna May Wong and a great deal of luggage. E. R. Richee's portrait of the star in the same costume handsomely delineates her "haughtily mysterious face."

Rolling stock for *Shanghai Express* was borrowed from the Santa Fe Railroad and shunted to Paramount's lot. While waiting for a set-up to be completed, director Von Sternberg rests on a packing case (*above*). A familiar military note is struck when Dietrich "suddenly claps Clive Brook's army cap on her head" (*right*). In a publicity still for the film (*opposite*), photographer Don English managed to get into the picture.

part of her imply the whole of her. Instead of showing Shanghai Lily at prayer, asking God to spare her lover's life, he photographs only her hands, pressed together in the carriage's darkness but illuminated by moonlight like nervous white shoots pushing their way up from some long-buried patch of faith. It reminds one of a similar shot in Dietrich's late German film, *Ship of Lost Souls*.

Shanghai Express is remembered for its freakish sound as well as its dazzling photography (which won Lee Garmes that year's Oscar). Von Sternberg had the perverse notion of making everyone aboard speak in a bizarre slowed-up monotone like an early phonograph sluggishly running down. "They talk like a train," was how he contemptuously answered what he regarded as a redundant query at the press conference. But the sound compels us to listen closely and be struck by Dietrich's equally bizarre pronunciation. In her films generally, she is no match for Garbo when it comes to verbal idiosyncrasies. One can nearly always accurately anticipate how Dietrich will speak a line: she demands attention with her veiled and faintly callous voice, but yields no major surprises—except in this film, in the famous line, "It took more than one man to change my name to Shanghai Lily." She gives the word "Shanghai" an acoustically exotic first syllable and a strangely pendulous final one so that it comes out of her lips like "Chung-high-yee." It is a growling boast that makes one feel that "Shanghai Lily" ought to be the name of a battle honor awarded posthumously to the men who fought over Dietrich and perished in the bold endeavor.

The military note is plangently struck throughout the film. Even in her spiky black plumes Dietrich finds a chance to assume soldier's gear. No surprise in the film is more beautiful than the moment when, clad in an extravagantly feminine stole trimmed with fox fur and fully ten feet long, she suddenly claps Clive Brook's army cap on her head, like a badge of loyalty, and imparts a rakish tilt to it like a salute from a woman whose love is based on the same code of chivalry as her soldier man's. In the film's last image, as they kiss, Brook surrenders his officer's gloves and whip to her embracing grasp—perhaps Von Sternberg's own perverse joke, considering how *he* retained the whip hand over his leading lady.

But if we are to believe him (always a questionable assumption), Von Sternberg was by this time reluctant to make any more films with Dietrich. "After *Dishonored*, I was finished," he said, "but Miss Dietrich said to me, 'You want to show the world that you're a great director and I'm a bad actress. Isn't that what you want to do? You want me to go to another director?'" He had given in to her: perhaps he would have us believe that he, too, was a gentleman at heart. His merciful attitude, fortified by a hefty salary rise, helped him to continue to "paint the Lily" in *Shanghai Express*.

The critics, too, colored it with praise. "Miss Dietrich gives an impressive performance," said Mordaunt Hall in the *New York Times*. "She is a languorous and fearless Lily ... she measures every word and yet she is not slow in her foreign accented speech." The unnamed critic of the London *Times* was to add at the film's opening in England: "Her acting finds its strength and impulse in her careful elimination of all emphasis, and the more seemingly careless and inconsequential her gestures, the more surely do they reveal the particular shades and movements of her mind."

But evidence begins to collect at this point in her career that Dietrich was fast wearying—if not already sick—of the image of the "tart with a heart of steel" (in Sheridan Morley's phrase) and wanted to humanize her screen character. Arriving in London, in March 1931, for the premiere there of *Morocco*, she was already inquiring, "Why do people call me a Greta Garbo? Why do they associate my name eternally with lovemaking? I have met Greta Garbo. I have seen her films. We are not the slightest bit alike. I do not concentrate on lovemaking on the screen. I am as happy to play the part of a charwoman. . . . Is lovemaking more interesting than domestication? Both are an art. I suppose they should come naturally. I cannot explain my 'recipes'—I have not any."[28] A few months later, in a signed *Saturday Review* article, she was insisting,

I want to play interesting women with many sides to their characters, because I believe that in creating a variety of characters the individuality of the actress herself becomes richer and deeper. I am determined to assert my own personality and to remain detached as far as possible from the popular conception of the vamp. Perhaps my resentment of this unfair method of exploitation has added a certain piquancy to the wry, mocking smile I assumed for my world-weary heroines.

In a series published in a fan magazine by Gerda Huber, an intimate from her Berlin days whom Dietrich had imported to Hollywood to be little Maria's companion and governess, Dietrich admitted that "without [Von Sternberg] I should be absolutely nothing . . . he is the one and only man who is capable of bringing out my true self." At which, her husband interjects, "That self is a born mother."

If that is true, then Von Sternberg cannot be said to have played the midwife very noticeably—until their new film together, *Blonde Venus* (1932). The subject is a mother's affection for her child. Or so it is made to appear, and probably did so appear to ordinary filmgoers. But this orthodox emotion is inextricably enmeshed with the mother's darker inclination, when the bills have to be paid for her ailing husband's medical treatment, to accept and even invite sexual enslavement by a rich protector and enter into the spirit and the company of a round of nightclub acts with sado-masochistic trappings. Von Sternberg has done two stealthy things here. He has taken details of his own early experiences, generally to do with the humiliations experienced in ghetto life in Europe and America, and combined them with a story that almost parodies Dietrich's own career as an entertainer who abandons a weak-willed husband (though taking her child with her) for the material luxury and artistic fulfillment that a man of the world can offer.

The movie contains two of her most farfetched singing acts. One is the gorilla-into-lady number of "Hot Voodoo," in which she comes on stage totally disguised in a hairy carapace that makes her look like a disconcertingly realistic relative of King Kong's. This gorilla suit she proceeds to peel off in a barbaric

version of a striptease, first revealing a slender arm encircled with glittering bracelets and finally emerging in a sequined body garment, long net stockings, with feathers sprouting banderilla-like from her waist, and all topped by an albino-hued fuzzy-wuzzy wig. "All night long I don't know right from wrong," she brazenly claims, while her pose, reminiscent of *The Blue Angel*, one leg up on a chair while the other supports her like a pale and slender pillar, testifies to Von Sternberg's love affair with the erotically predatory paintings of Klimt. Later, in white tailcoat and matching topper, she marches through a Paris cabaret number with lesbian-like swagger.

Such numbers remain more visually striking than vocally effective, for a good reason: the Sam Coslow-Ralph Rainger songs which Dietrich sings lack the decadent resonance of Friedrich (or Frederick, as he later became) Holländer's. The film's setting in Depression-hit America is inhospitable to Dietrich's glamorous creation, supposedly down on her luck and holing up in flophouses. The thought of Dietrich (of all people!) having a rough time, with all her assets, is simply, well, unthinkable—her slumming becomes, willy nilly, a sort of royal progress undertaken *incognita* by choice rather than *de rigueur*. Von Sternberg was also unable to smuggle his usual charge of eroticism past the strengthened morality code that Hollywood had lately adopted. Although the executives in the Paramount front office had trouble locating any precise cause for their moral concern, the relationship between mother and child in the film was disturbing. A child was usually put into a scenario as a sop to the censors, since an erring mother who took her child along with her on her trip into turpitude had her guilty conscience pricked by its constant presence, and it was a handicap to any immoral opportunities that came Mama's way among the men in her life.

But Dietrich and Garbo are two stars who impart curious undertones to their scenes with children: they portray motherhood in a way that flatters the latent manhood of the child they are petting, dressing or bathing. The child actors, in consequence, have an involuntary but precocious sexuality thrust on them. Paramount finally seized on one particular scene, where Dietrich temporarily stowed her child away under a restaurant table, while inviting the interest of men, as an excuse for demanding cuts in the scenario. Von Sternberg refused to make them. He was replaced by Richard Wallace, a director of B-pictures. Then it was Dietrich's turn to walk off the picture. Before the affair was settled, Von Sternberg was threatened with a $100,000 damages suit and Dietrich with replacement by Tallulah Bankhead. (Characteristically, Von Sternberg accused Paramount of undervaluing his services!)

A threat which Dietrich considered more alarming than Tallulah Bankhead occurred while she was still on suspension. In May 1932, she received a warning that unless she paid over $10,000, harm would befall little Maria. In the wake of the Lindbergh baby's kidnapping, this threat had to be taken seriously. Dietrich increased to six the number of bodyguards at her North Roxbury Drive home in Beverly Hills, and her chauffeur was armed. Nothing came of the threat—except a

In London for the British première of *Morocco* at the Carlton Cinema.

The heroine of *Blonde Venus* had little in common with the classical Greek ideal of womanhood, but for the film's release in Germany the poster artist reshaped Dietrich's slender hips and thighs to heighten her resemblance to the Venus de Milo (*opposite*). The movie contains two visually striking singing sequences: a gorilla-into-lady striptease (*right*) and a cabaret number in white tailcoat and matching topper.

The young Cary Grant played a supporting role in *Blonde Venus* as a wealthy man-about-town who becomes Marlene's protector (*above*), only to discover that his inamorata has wandered off the straight and narrow in order to support her son and ailing husband. Even in her scenes with the child (Dickie Moore, *right*), Dietrich "flatters the latent manhood of the child."

not unuseful amount of publicity for a star on suspension—but the security measures put unwelcome pressures on family life.

That there were already some pressures was indicated in later years by Maria's own account of her childhood which she gave to the *Ladies Home Journal* in 1951. Her bodyguards, she said, for the most part kind, fatherly men, were the only friends she had, though the household boasted two tutors (one English, one German), a governess, a butler, maids, and the pistol-packing chauffeur. Maria was proud that her mother never treated her like a daughter. Mother and child behaved to each other like friends, and the child discussed Dietrich's clothes, visited her on the set, read her scripts, and "as I matured, I was often taken for her sister, an older sister because I was so heavy" (Maria developed some psychosomatic weight problems). "I have always felt the older one in the relationship," she added. She had lots of animals—a German shepherd dog (for security again), a monkey, several cats, two sheep, a parrot and an aviary with 200 birds. Dietrich threw parties twice a week. But Maria also recalled that she "resented the fact that we could not be together more. When mother was working, she would go to bed at eight o'clock. When she was not working, she would go out evenings, dressed in jewels and furs. I just wanted her to stand there, shimmering and perfumed only for me, but I knew she was dressing for someone else. . . . I would cry myself to sleep in the dark."[29] Even mother's beauty was confusing: "I never felt good enough for her. She was so beautiful that it always gave me a feeling of ugliness and unworthiness."

Where Dietrich got the huge amount of money she needed to live in the style she did is a minor mystery. Yes, she was certainly very highly paid: but her outgoings were heavy, so were taxes levied on the wealthy, especially after Roosevelt became president and the New Deal's fiscal laws began to bite. Contrary to general belief, a film studio is frequently very stingy about allowing its stars to "charge it up" when it comes to a lavish life-style; and the Internal Revenue could be even tougher—in one recorded instance, Joan Crawford's claim for a wardrobe allowance was checked (and rejected) by a Revenue man visiting the MGM studios to vet with a magnifying glass every still displaying the star in a costume that represented a tax claim by her. Dietrich always made a point of living for today, never tomorrow: perhaps she spent the money as fast as it came in during those good years. Perhaps she also enjoyed a secret arrangement— secret from the other Paramount contract artists—whereby she got a percentage of the net earnings on her pictures. In my researches into Garbo in the MGM archives, just such an arrangement was disclosed as having been negotiated in total and lasting secrecy around this time (1932) for this star. Dietrich was also represented by Garbo's agent, Harry Edington, who was one of the few Gentiles practicing his sharp-witted trade in Hollywood, and much favored by stars who believed that Edington and his partner Frank Vincent had a special *entrée* to the predominantly Jewish movie industry just because of their unorthodox status. Whatever the truth about her money, Dietrich was well looked after.

Living it up in Hollywood. Dietrich had a suitably lavish home in Beverly Hills with a large retinue of servants, including for a while six bodyguards. In between films she would get caught up in the movie colony's social whirl. Premières provided a never-ending opportunity for photographers to snap the stars in their finery. *Right, above*: Rouben Mamoulian, Jean Harlow, Dietrich and Von Sternberg; *right, below*: Maurice Chevalier, Dietrich and Gary Cooper.

She had widened her circle of friends, somewhat to Von Sternberg's nervous annoyance. He tried, unsuccessfully, to ban the publication of a *paparazzi*-type photo of Dietrich and Maurice Chevalier dancing cheek to cheek at the Coconut Grove. But she struck up an even closer relationship with Garbo's intimate friend, Mercedes de Acosta, a Hollywood screenwriter, authoress and socialite with a penchant for being accepted as the confidante of female movie stars. In her memoirs, Mercedes de Acosta recounts how this attraction was reciprocated when Dietrich unexpectedly turned up on her doorstep, gaining admittance with some familiar phrases to her German maid, and presenting De Acosta with a huge bouquet of white tuberoses. As the hostess extended a gratified hand in welcome, Dietrich took it with a significant gesture: "In an almost military manner [she] bent over it and firmly shook it." The two women were of instant service to each other: Dietrich expressed her *Hausfrau*'s compulsion to cook for someone whom she had thought undernourished when she first saw her, and De Acosta in turn says she persuaded Dietrich to cleanse the rouge off her cheeks and adopt a paler and more interesting shade of white. She also took credit for putting Dietrich into slacks: but here she was undoubtedly overstating her case. The two remained firm friends, exchanging costly gifts almost weekly: flowers (sometimes twice daily) from Dietrich until even De Acosta demurred, whereupon she switched to giving vases, and receiving books and paintings in return. So far as is known, though, De Acosta never succeeded in bringing Dietrich and Garbo together socially.

Not everyone was a Dietrich fan, however. An anti-Dietrich coterie was not long in making itself visible and vocal, baited by the Svengali-Trilby-like relationship of Von Sternberg and his star. That particular theme had been expressed in two well-publicized John Barrymore movies which opened just as Dietrich's Hollywood career moved into overdrive: one was Archie Mayo's film *Svengali*, the other Michael Curtiz's *The Mad Genius,* about a Russian impresario who dominates a ballerina. The first was released in May 1931, the second in October. Thus the Von Sternberg-Dietrich relationship inspired anticipatory reverberations of the same kind as each of their new films neared release: the complicity of their talents, hinting at a vague but potent domination of one by the other, was a bonus to the publicists. Not always, though, to the two talents themselves. *Vanity Fair* wrote of Von Sternberg in 1932 that he "traded his . . . style for fancy play chiefly upon the legs in silk, the buttocks in lace, of Dietrich, of whom he has made a paramount [*sic*] slut." And John Grierson, the respected British critic and filmmaker, directed one of his most famous and acerbic phrases, "When a director dies, he becomes a cameraman," at Von Sternberg's *Shanghai Express*.

Fan magazines, which depended on access to the stars, rarely fell out with powerful studios. But the November 1931 issue of *Photoplay* published a wicked lampoon of a "typical day" in Dietrich's life that bites deeply and accurately enough to warrant reprinting today. The satirist Leonard Hall clearly relished the blood he drew.

Marlene Dietrich is essentially a "home girl." The famous German star, shy and retiring in company, which she seldom is in, said today, "I am happiest among my kiddie. Also among my hubby and my book. I am also extremely happy among my saucepan. Ach, you should taste my *pfann-kuchen und kartoffel-salat*. Also my *strudel*. I am very very happy among my *strudel*. And I like to be alone.

Hall described part of an imagined crowded afternoon's shooting on a movie entitled *Below the Equator*:

1.00 p.m. Back on the set. Miss Dietrich is now wearing a cherry-colored sun bonnet with coral piping and an insert of turkey-red fichu. The scene is a nightclub in Panama City. Marlene is playing twenty-four Albertina Rausch dancing girls, thus showing no less than forty-eight perfect Dietrich legs at one and the same time. . . . Cinematographer Lee Garmes has sixty-six cameras focused on the set, some of them shooting through lace, cellophane, cobwebs. . . . Von Sternberg dismisses the troupe by firing a field-gun and running up the Von Sternberg house flag.

2.30 p.m. Retakes of scenes showing Miss Dietrich's ears, neck, elbows and torso. These were taken in error by an assistant director while Von Sternberg was out seeing a lady about an Airedale. Scenes are substituted displaying Miss Dietrich's knees, thighs, ankles, arches, great toes and shin bones. "Looks like a great audience picture," murmurs the crowd, now numbering 4,000.

3.00 p.m. Miss Dietrich poses for still photographs at the studio. Among the poses shot is one with Miss Dietrich with an arm round her little girl, while her little girl has her arm around her daddy and her daddy has his arm around Mr. von Sternberg's throat.

To receive this love-hate treatment so early in her American career shows how widely the whole operatic set-up of compliant star and her overweening director had established itself in the imagination of the public and the media. The Von Sternberg-Dietrich films generated the kind of synergism, or mutually advantageous friction, that was worth a platoon of movie publicists. At least they did at first.

While *Blonde Venus* was dying at the box office, despite valiant publicity efforts, an unconcerned Von Sternberg was touring the West Indies trying to find a hurricane to photograph as "background" for his next Dietrich film—as yet it existed only in his mind. So with her mentor's agreement—for her contract required his agreement to such a "loan-out"—she started making *The Song of Songs* (1933) under a Von Sternberg-approved director, Rouben Mamoulian. It was an adaptation of a Sudermann story filmed twice already. A peasant girl turns artist's model, becomes a baroness, then sinks into what was politely termed "bohemia" as a cabaret artist: such a plot could have been made to fit Dietrich's *persona* by only one man—and he was at present hunting hurricanes in the Caribbean. "Joe, where are you?" Dietrich whispered into the microphone as each day's shooting began. She had tried to avoid doing the film on reading the screenplay, but a lawsuit threatening to hit her for $180,000 if she did so managed to change her mind.

But more to the point, Paramount had even sought an injunction restraining Dietrich from leaving America until she did the film or paid the forfeit. It really was believed that she intended going back to Germany, bringing her new international stardom with her as collateral for her own production company

With Von Sternberg on a temporary leave of absence, Rouben Mamoulian took over as director of Dietrich's next film, *Song of Songs*. The character she plays undergoes various transformations. Early in the film Dietrich appears as an assistant in her aunt's bookshop, where she encounters a young sculptor (Brian Aherne, peeping from behind a book, *opposite*). Later she becomes a baroness. Unit photographer Don English has caught her in the latter guise (*opposite, below*) resting on the set, while director Mamoulian confers with the script girl. Dietrich is taking it easy as well in the contraption below, designed to allow actresses to relax without creasing their costumes.

WATCH YOUR STEP

inside the UFA set-up, perhaps with Von Sternberg as director-in-perpetuity. She herself had fed this suspicion. Maybe it was just part of the politics of Hollywood contract-making—more likely, it was sheer indiscretion—which caused her to say, as she reclined on a *chaise longue* in Von Sternberg's office during an interview she granted a magazine journalist in March 1932, "I want to go back to Germany. I have had good roles here. I suppose I might be said to have done well. [One hears the sound of her master's sarcasm in this mock humility.] But I want to work in my own country and in my own language. I think I shall go home for good next Christmas when my contract is up." The interviewer, picking up the point of her earlier refusing to work for anyone else but Von Sternberg, began, "But when you go back to Germany . . ." She interrupted: "I have not thought so far ahead . . . Mr. von Sternberg's contract expires at the same time. He wants to tour the Far East. I don't know. We shall see."[30]

Paramount was an organization that *did* look far ahead: very far ahead when its financial self-interest was involved. It kept Von Sternberg under secret surveillance when he went to Germany early in 1933—*that* was where Joe was, in answer to Dietrich's rhetorical question on the *Song of Songs* set: doing some very practical haggling with UFA. That he may have failed to set up a production company for Dietrich and himself is a matter of historical inevitability rather than frustrated desire. Hitler became Chancellor in January 1933 and was voted full powers by the Reichstag in March. Jewish film people were packing their bags even earlier to set out on the great diaspora of the 1930s which enriched the Hollywood and (for a time under Korda) the British film industries with talented refugees. Dietrich would have been a welcome ornament in the new Reich—though, as she soon made plain, she would never have consented to adorning Hitler's artists' gallery. But Von Sternberg's Jewish origins would have almost certainly disqualified him from directing Dietrich, or anyone else for that matter.

It was apprehension for her family that may have explained the withdrawn air Dietrich possessed when passing through New York en route to Europe in May 1933. At least one journalist contrasted the "indifference" of "the exotic German star" with the "totally unsophisticated, very bright, charmingly natural" girl who had chattered away to the press on first arriving in America in 1930.

The German press took an increasingly strident tone of disapproval towards Dietrich in the next few years, although, as Von Ribbentrop, the Nazi envoy in London, told her in 1936, "this can be reversed at twenty-four hours' notice." *The Song of Songs* was banned in Germany, ostensibly on moral grounds; and Dietrich returned to Hollywood in September 1933. She was not to revisit Germany until 1945, though her family stayed there under the Nazis.

So, for her, it was back to Von Sternberg; both of them had new contracts. His next scenario was based on Catherine the Great's rise to power as Empress of Russia being interpreted not in territorial terms alone, but as destructive sexuality. This is what one had missed in *The Song of Songs*: the Dietrich of that film had no masculine grain in her nature. She had nothing to play her looks against.

Dietrich returned to her native Germany for a brief visit in the summer of 1933. En route back to Hollywood in September, she was photographed in the vestibule of her Pullman car, wearing the calf-length skirt that was just then coming into fashion.

The Song of Songs's principal interest resides in the way it compels us to see a star illuminated by the *absence* of such qualities and so measure the difference between Dietrich and someone like Garbo whose sexual ambiguity remained an alloy that even the most banal story could not dissolve into mere decorative femininity.

There is a very curious parallel between Garbo's film subjects and Dietrich's which suggests that each studio, MGM and Paramount, was keeping a close eye on the other's star. For Garbo's *Mata Hari* there is Dietrich's *Dishonored*; for *Grand Hotel* there is *Shanghai Express* (which is *Grand Hotel* on wheels); for *Susan Lenox:Her Fall and Rise* there is *Blonde Venus*; and for *Queen Christina* there is the Catherine the Great project entitled *The Scarlet Empress* (1934).

But putting Dietrich back into historical dress served a more short-term purpose than inviting comparison with Greta Garbo. The newly formed Roman Catholic National Legion of Decency was holding preliminary meetings in 1933 before officially constituting itself the following year as a pressure group capable of imposing a box-office boycott on morally offensive films. The move struck at the basis of the character which Dietrich had so often played, in fact or symbol: namely the contemporary prostitute in the lightly redeeming guise of cabaret entertainer, patriotic spy, cast-off mother or artist's model. The solution found was to dress up the whore in historical costume, set her on a throne instead of in a brothel (though the circumstances of the Russian imperial court are ambiguous enough to pass for such) and still surround her with well-endowed men—though this time the men are *hers* to hire and the terms on which they ostensibly serve her are military, not commercial.

A militaristic autocracy guarded by oversized soldiery proved a striking setting for Dietrich's courtesan empress; and the male uniform she slips on for her *coup d'état*, with a white cavalry shako doing duty for the customary white topper of her transvestite cabaret uniform, confirmed her fidelity to the "officer and gentleman" ethic. Now she is the centerpiece of a baroque court ruled by the crazed whims of a prematurely senile Grand Duke (actor Sam Jaffe, scuttering from behind tapestries and sculptured gargoyles like an obscene white mole) and a vertiginous camera on its crane adding a patterned feeling of hide-and-seek to the conspiracies of love, power and perversion. The film contains one of the half-dozen greatest lighting effects in cinema: Catherine the Great reviewing her officers and melting into the shadows, the spotlighted white of one eye a diminishing point of roguishness to the end of the fade-out. There is also the wondrously suggestive effect contributed by her bridal veil. At first its fine mesh screens the wolfish cavities out of her cheeks and, aided by a glycerined tear, transforms her into an icon madonna: later the coarser net curtaining around her bed, and the glint of a teardrop diamond she is fondling against her cheek, restore the hardness to her looks and suggest the harsh rule of the future Empress of Russia.

The fact that Dietrich is seen seducing only one guardsman is no attempt on Von Sternberg's part to whitewash history, simply an acknowledgment that

The screen careers of Garbo and Dietrich went closely in tandem. Garbo's *Queen Christina* (1933, with John Gilbert, *above*) was followed one year later by Dietrich's Catherine the Great in *Scarlet Empress* (*below*, with Gavin Gordon).

MΛRLENE
DIETRICH
in
THE SCΛRLET
EMPRESS
with
JOHN LODGE SAM JAFFE & LOUISE DRESSER
Directed by
JOSEF VON STERNBERG
RELEASE
DATE SEPT.10 1934

Paramount
Pictures

The "wondrously suggestive effect contributed by her bridal veil" in Von Sternberg's film (*opposite, below*) contrasts with the studio artist's coarser portrait of Dietrich as the future Empress. Early in the film, the actress is seen as an innocent and timorous German princess (*below*, flanked by John Lodge and C. Aubrey Smith), but soon she is immersed in the luxury and intrigue of the Russian court, with only her beauty and wits to sustain her (*left*).

Joseph Breen, czar in his own right of the Hollywood Morality Code, has his eye on the Empress. Dietrich's sexuality is constantly filtered through the exercise of destructive power. The frightened virgin princess who turns into a military autocrat determinedly riding up the palace steps on her horse simply confirms the power she has learned to exercise in the bedchamber. The film has an unusual interest, though, in requiring Dietrich at the start to sink her established personality into a character which is visibly not like hers. She had done this before when she played a simple peasant in *The Song of Songs*, but not so effectively as in her portrayal of the timorous *ingénue* chosen to be the foreign bride of the Grand Duke in *The Scarlet Empress*. Von Sternberg sends her scuttling around the court in ribbons, bib and tucker, looking in the words of Cecil Beaton—who did not intend it as a compliment—"as if she had fallen into a baby's bassinet." She is helped of course by very tender lighting, very "young" hairstyles: but her nervous, jumpy rhythm is anti-Dietrich, and a revelation. It is one of the few times when Von Sternberg required her to *act* a role, not just lend herself to his fabrication of personality and atmosphere.

But if Dietrich's patience had not diminished, that of the people whom Paramount hoped would see the film had. Alexander Korda's rival film, *Catherine the Great*, with Elisabeth Bergner, had been premiered in America in February 1934. Von Sternberg's picture, covering exactly the same ground, was held back until September. The British film was all straight storytelling; the American one, it seemed to its critics, was all self-indulgence. They complained of the director's "narcotic influence" on the players. "A.D.S." (André Sennwald), in the *New York Times*, said he had "even accomplished the improbable feat of smothering the enchanting Marlene Dietrich under his technique, although his camerawork . . . never does her less than justice."[31] Richard Watts, Jr., in the *Herald Tribune*, was not so merciful: "Under his tutelage, Miss Dietrich has become a hapless sort of automaton."[32] Despite barbaric decor and grotesque pageantry, the film's fate was sealed, as far as popular audiences were concerned, by its failure *as story*.

Sam Jaffe, the Paramount executive, recalls a curious slip of the tongue on Von Sternberg's part which suggests the extent to which he felt himself committed not just to the "art film" but to the silent art film, which is what *The Scarlet Empress* recalls, since it has scarcely a single effect or plot point that depends on sound—which is a compliment to it. The director once mentioned "titles" to Jaffe, who realized what he was referring to and said, "Joe, they don't call them 'titles' now, they call them 'dialogue.'" It would be an interesting experiment to run *The Scarlet Empress* without its sound dialogue track, using only music and the appropriate written silent-film "dialogue" titles. The film would probably work as well.

The last film which Von Sternberg made with Dietrich was even more consciously a return to the past. He described *The Devil Is a Woman* (1935) as "a final tribute to the lady I had seen lean against the wings of a Berlin stage five years earlier." The *femme fatale* of *The Blue Angel* reappears as "Concha the savage . . . the

Following the box-office failure of the historically costumed *Scarlet Empress,* Paramount ordered this high-fashion portrait by William Walling, Jr., to help publicize the star's next film.

toast of Spain," who humiliates her men for no other reason than perversity. Von Sternberg, as if sensing that this would be his last opportunity to enjoy the masochistic pleasure of it all, cast Lionel Atwill as her victim, a *Doppelgänger* not only resembling in uncanny detail Von Sternberg's own appearance, with his droopy mustache and dandified costume, but even possessing the director's curt and ironic manner of speaking. The story is told by him (the "director figure") in flashback as a series of tense confrontations (such as Von Sternberg favored in his directing) frequently set in a carnival atmosphere (akin to the make-believe of a film studio) and dealing with a love-hate relationship (such as a star and her director engender). It is, all told, a better autobiography than the one Von Sternberg was to write years later.

It is the self-lacerating tone that is so disturbing. For outside *The Blue Angel*, Von Sternberg composed no more heartless a series of degradations than that which he makes his proxy victim suffer in *The Devil Is A Woman*, as Dietrich plucks a cigarette from Atwill's lips and bestows it on the gigolo he has surprised her entertaining, pays the young man for his services with a bill from her protector's wallet, and sends him off with a flower broken off the bouquet that Atwill himself has brought her. This cruel ceremony has military undertones, too: it is like the public degradation inflicted on a court-martialed officer whose buttons, medals and other insignia are stripped off on the parade ground before he is dismissed the service. When Atwill declares his love for her despite all this, Dietrich's retort is like a dagger which Von Sternberg the director has turned against himself: "You have always mistaken vanity for love."

It must be said that the film does not carry the sense of vengeance over into its handsome looks. Dietrich had never appeared more ravishing. As if finally to "sign" his creation, Von Sternberg took a photography credit, too. Dietrich always considered it her favorite film, because it was the most "beautiful" one she had made—and, she would ask, is "beauty" not what life is all about? Well, not quite.

"Miss Dietrich and I have progressed as far as possible together," the director informed the press a few days before he finished shooting. "My being with her in future will not help her or me." Dietrich made it clear that "I didn't leave Mr. von Sternberg . . . he left me . . . I was not very happy about that."[33]

Von Sternberg left Paramount for Columbia Pictures, where, showing a self-interest that transcended old feuds, B. P. Schulberg (who had also come over from Paramount) engaged him to make two pictures. But this volatile, arrogant man worked only intermittently until his death in 1969—the last of the directors who, as Flora Robson was to say during the aborted filming of his English epic *I, Claudius*, "came on the set dressed as if he was going to appear in his pictures." And with his departure from Paramount, Von Sternberg's "Dietrich" ceased to exist, too. The flesh-and-blood original was now inherited by Ernst Lubitsch, whose contract empowered him to produce his own films as well as supervise all the studio's.

In *The Devil Is a Woman*, the last Dietrich-Von Sternberg collaboration, "the *femme fatale* of *The Blue Angel* reappears as 'Concha the Savage . . . the toast of Spain'." It was Dietrich's favorite film.

Dietrich's victim in *The Devil Is a Woman* is played by Lionel Atwill (*below*, recovering from a duel wound), made up to resemble Von Sternberg's own appearance "in uncanny detail."

Von Sternberg's departure from Paramount did not rupture Dietrich's relationship with the studio. In this photo of 1935, she is surrounded by various Paramount executives, including Ernst Lubitsch (far right), who produced her next film.

Dietrich's "emancipation" is immediately evident in *Desire* (1936), which Lubitsch produced and Frank Borzage directed. "For the first time [in an American film]," wrote Frank Nugent in the *New York Times*, "she is permitted to walk, breathe, smile and shrug as a human being instead of being a canvas for the Louvre"[34]—a snide reference, perhaps, to a Paramount publicity photo which superimposed Dietrich's enigmatic features on the Mona Lisa's. (She was also portrayed, androgynously, as a stand-in for Gainsborough's portrait of *The Blue Boy*.) Dietrich found *Desire* a liberating experience. It was a present-day story, to start with, and lighter in tone than any she had been used to since her German comedies. She played a high-class jewel thief who has to flirt with a (not too) serious young American-in-Europe (Gary Cooper) in order to retrieve the stolen bauble she has smuggled out of France inside his baggage. Borzage was a director with no interest in touching any of the darker bases of sexuality. The mood of the film was engaging: it wanted to make its people likable; and since the slight story weighed no one down, the cast responded with spirit.

Dietrich always called it the easiest film she ever made and her reasons, significantly, harked back to the days of subordination she had suffered under Von Sternberg. "Until *Desire*, I have always had to conceal my feelings and still show that I loved the man, whoever he was. This is the most difficult thing of all. Nothing is easier to play than straight sentiments. Mr. von Sternberg never let me play love scenes—not ordinary ones, I mean, with hugging and all that, because he hates ordinary love scenes. In *Morocco*, Gary Cooper was supposed to kiss me, but behind a fan. That was all."[35] *Desire* thus broke another taboo that predated Von Sternberg: namely the slap on the face that Dietrich's mother had delivered when her daughter turned up her nose at dancing with a boy she didn't like. At long last she could show her feelings without being accused of bad manners.

The film's production values also helped a "new" Dietrich emerge. Travis Banton, the studio's brilliant wardrobe designer, gave her a simpler line, producing a *cuisine minceur* effect in dress where formerly there had been a banquet. In the opinion of Eugenia Sheppard, women's features editor of the New York *Herald Tribune* in the 1960s, Dietrich's double-breasted sports jacket worn in the film over a white dress was an outdoor costume that "marked the beginning of today's good taste." Such details brought her closer to the audiences than Von Sternberg would ever have thought desirable. The Frederick Hollander-Leo Robin composition she sang at the piano expressed by its very title that the days of somnambulism were over—"Awake in a Dream," it was called.

Contemporary reality, however, was not to be taken too far. Dietrich was next rushed into a remake of Pola Negri's 1927 success *Hotel Imperial*, retitled in Lubitsch's typically frivolous vein as *I Loved a Soldier*. She was entrusted to the director Henry Hathaway, who had just done the *amour fou* film to end them all, *Peter Ibbetson*, with Gary Cooper. But his strategy now was to appeal to Dietrich's *Hausfrau* side, specifying that the film would open with her on her knees scrubbing the floor in the hotel where she shelters the fugitive soldier. As love grew between them, Dietrich was to be transformed: she would cleanse the smudges off her cheeks, change her soiled chambermaid's uniform, redo her hair, apply makeup and have achieved an unearthly beauty by the time of her wedding, which was to take place in a cathedral.

But these plans for graduated grooming were apparently subverted by what, from now on, became an increasingly overbearing aspect of Dietrich's way of working. Von Sternberg had left her a legacy in the shape of his fanatical attention to detail: this she duly inherited and now she set about "projecting" the image she wanted of herself with truly Prussian strength of will. Lubitsch fell out with Paramount's management during the film. He stepped down from managing the studio and, according to Hathaway, "with [him] gone, she misbehaved." Whatever the truth, it seems the slovenly chrysalid that was to disgorge the exquisite creature was relegated more and more to the background. Hathaway would say, "You're not supposed to be beautiful till next Thursday." Dietrich would respond, "Please—can't it be at least Wednesday?" Eventually she used a contract clause specifying that Lubitsch must be the producer of the film. As he wasn't, she quit; it was never finished.

This example of her artistic obstinacy should not surprise us. She was no sooner freed from Von Sternberg than she began exercising more than her independence—she began applying in the most immediate and practical form all the technique she had learned from that master. He had given her everything she

In *Desire*, a "new" and more contemporary Dietrich emerged. Some twenty-five years later, Eugenia Sheppard was to describe the star's double-breasted sports jacket worn over a white dress as "the beginning of today's good taste." Dietrich was also allowed for the first time to play "ordinary love scenes" (*below*, with Gary Cooper).

Moments in the making of a movie: measuring the distance for focus (*opposite*) and reviewing stills with *Desire*'s director, Frank Borzage (*left*). Dietrich's *Hausfrau* side was to be featured in *I Loved a Soldier* (*below*), but the film was never completed with Dietrich in the role.

needed to protect her essential personality, *as she saw it*, and also to project its physical image to the very best advantage. The Dietrich of the later years who demanded the obedient execution of her orders down to the last detail took shape—and quickly—during this period. Her authoritative nature had lain more or less dormant during Von Sternberg's reign, though witnesses reported hearing them have their differences (arguments usually conducted in staccato German), invariably about technique, not interpretation. But from this time on, references proliferate in published interviews and private memoranda to Dietrich's "way of doing things."

This "way" was first felt in *The Garden of Allah* (1936). It was Dietrich's first film as a "loan out" from Paramount to the independent producer David O. Selznick. Selznick was also a politician of restless guile, who calculated the advantages that could come from exaggerating the shortcomings of any star he was interested in signing. A contrite performer, suitably humbled by Selznick's evaluation of his or her services, would be of a mind to accept less—so he figured. Accordingly, he told Gregory Ratoff, the Russian-born actor who was his go-between with Dietrich, that he would be pleased to have her in his film, but she must recognize that "any sales manager or important theater man will tell you—and indeed will tell her, if he is honest—that she has been hurt to such a terrible extent that she is no longer even a fairly important box-office star. . . . She is in no position to command a fabulous salary."[36] At least, not from "Honest" Dave.

Her agent, Harry Edington, was equal to this ploy. He used the Selznick offer (at a reduced price) as bait to catch a bigger fish. By the time Dietrich had signed with Selznick for *The Garden of Allah*, she was already committed to making *Knight Without Armor* in England for Alexander Korda at a fee reported to be not less than $450,000, a huge remuneration for the time.

This *coup* actually had the effect of reassuring Selznick. If Dietrich had to report to Denham Studios, England, at a prearranged date, maybe it would curb her rumored penchant for "interfering," as far as his production was concerned. But he added in one of his memos: "Maybe I am just naive!" What happened, in fact, was that two temperaments, each with a compulsion to control the minutiae of production, clashed over this film. Soon Selznick's telegrams to director Richard Boleslawski, who was shooting on location in the Arizona desert, became extremely short-tempered. "It is high time for a showdown . . . I wish you would lose your temper [with her and Charles Boyer] and I will have a lot more respect for you if you turn into a Von Sternberg who tolerates no interference."[37]

All this throws a most interesting light on Dietrich's passion for professionalism, which emerges in another not very well-known predilection of hers. In the previous few years she had made herself into one of Hollywood's most proficient home movie-makers, specializing in color photography. She had bought a Filmo 16mm. cine camera on one of her European visits, so as to make a record of Maria growing up. And long before *The Garden of Allah*, which was one of the earliest films to be shot in the improved three-color Technicolor process,

The *Garden of Allah* has Dietrich cast as an ex-convent girl who encounters an ex-monk (Charles Boyer, *left*) in the desert town of Beni-Mora. Much of the shooting was done on location near Yuma, Arizona. The film's director, Richard Boleslawski (with pipe, *below*), drank some of the desert water, caught an infection and died of it after shooting was completed.

she had made a Kodacolor test in secret for Paramount and been so impressed by it that she abandoned black-and-white in shooting home movies of her own, which she "produced" very expertly. In 1941 she told photographer William Stull that she possessed silent Kodacolor records of her Hollywood movies photographed "by Marlene Dietrich and associates." She often brought her cine camera to the studio, or on location, to record the scenes in which she herself did not appear. For the others, in which she figured, "I set the camera beforehand. Then when I step into the scene, I can always find someone—usually one of the assistant cameramen—who will shoot my scene for me, during a rehearsal, of course, so that the noise of my Filmo won't interfere with the 35mm. sound-recording."[38]

Asked which was the most interesting "personal" production she had made with her Filmo, Dietrich replied unhesitatingly: "One I made several years ago [in 1936, possibly] when my friend Josef von Sternberg was making a picture in Europe. I knew from his letters that he missed his beautiful home here in Hollywood. So I took my camera and lights, and went there, and made him a complete Kodacolor film of his home. . . . Mr. von Sternberg's home is beautiful and filled with exquisite works of art—paintings, statuary and the like. I photographed each of these pieces that were so dear to him, giving him close shots of each." She elaborated on the technical problems of avoiding glare from paintings while bringing out their individual textures. "Making this picture, and doing it so well technically and artistically that I could evoke praise from Mr. von Sternberg, not merely because of the sentimental nature of the subject matter, but because he—a truly great film craftsman—thought my photographic technique was in itself good, made that the most satisfying of all the 16mm. films I have made."

It is hard to think of another Hollywood star of that era, male or female, who had developed "technique" to such a professional pitch as Dietrich did in emulation of her mentor. No wonder the apprentice very quickly learned to fill the sorcerer's place and produce her own illusion!

She was certainly definite about what she wanted in *The Garden of Allah*. At first she wanted it to be shot in black-and-white. When Selznick insisted otherwise, she engaged Charles Lang, who had shot *Desire*, to do some Technicolor tests of her, as she had been appalled at what she considered the unappetizing results of other tests in that process. She commanded Lang (against the Technicolor people's wishes) to reduce the intense light then considered essential for color. When the test was printed, "its success," she said, "was known all over Hollywood in two hours." Circumstances made it impossible for Lang to photograph the Selznick picture, so Harold Rossen took his place with her approval. She then turned an eye on her costumes. "They told me I could not wear white because it was too glaring," she told the English journalist Charles Graves, during breaks in making the Korda film later that year, "but even in a black-and-white film which is badly lighted white is also glaring. I said to them, 'After all, the white in my eye

Dietrich was now an avid movie photographer herself. She would often bring her 16mm. camera on location (as here during the filming of *Garden of Allah*) to record mementos of the occasion.

photographs white, so why shouldn't I wear a white dress in a color film?'"[39]

A softer, more sentimental side of her nature was revealed once her lesson in logic had been absorbed. Maria, then aged eleven, was cast as a convent child in one scene because, as Dietrich said, "I wanted to have her in my first color film."

As things turned out, color was not *The Garden of Allah*'s best feature, though, as Dietrich observed, experiments were continuing two weeks into shooting and "at the end of the picture . . . it got better and better." No less a critic than the French writer Colette showed her repugnance for it in a rare film review: "Faced with the candied pink of [Dietrich's] cynical lip, the anemic gold of her hairstyle, the hesitant azure of her look, we hung fire." And Graham Greene wrote caustically of "the hideous Technicolor flowers, the yellow cratered desert like Gruyère cheese, the beige faces."

Even when she could not worry about the color of the Yuma locations, cheesy or not, she found other faults in the film, mainly to do with the dialogue. "Marlene's pictures have been notorious for their ghastly writing," Selznick exploded defensively. But for years afterwards, Dietrich had a succinct description ready for any interviewer rash enough to trespass on *The Garden of Allah*. It was, she said, "trash." It was indeed mystical hokum about an ex-convent girl and an ex-monk who meet each other in what is called "the face of the Infinite"—that Gruyère desert, it appears, more prosaically—but renounce all for the sake of God. Even Garbo, said Dietrich, would have been too canny to play in it—a "peasant" (*sic*) like her knew better than to send her lover back to a monastery at the fade-out. Dietrich's principal complaint was made on more refined grounds. "Many times," she said later, "I am embarrassed to tears by the things I have to say in films. . . . It is embarrassing to talk about God [in the middle of love scenes]. Imagine having to say, as I did, 'Nobody but God and I know what is in my heart.' The conceit of it! I tell you, I very nearly died!" It was the film that died instead.

The life Dietrich now led between films had settled into a well-ordered routine. Sometime during the year, she visited her husband in Paris; the rest of the time, she lived a semblance of an "open marriage," seemingly disregarding yet inevitably profiting from the curiosity and speculation evoked by her latest association with another celebrated figure.

These celebrity consorts fell into well-defined categories. First, there was the romantic screen idol who possessed a status comparable to her own. In the early 1930s, he was John Gilbert, just then past his peak but still a star who radiated the allure of the silent cinema that had given Dietrich herself her start. A little later, he was Douglas Fairbanks, Jr., particularly when Fairbanks was between marriages. In each case, Dietrich was attracted to a star whose screen roles were (or had been) filled with dash, ardor and all-for-love impulsiveness.

She also went for a second type of available man, the emphatically all-male exhibitionist, a character defined again and again in the he-man films of Howard Hawks. He is best represented by Ernest Hemingway, chauvinist to his heart's core, yet putting certain women on an equal footing with himself, willing to go ten rounds with them if they show a gutsy male nature inside their feminine exterior. Hemingway's term of endearment for Dietrich was "the Kraut," a sort of affectionate put-down between equals inviting a sock on the jaw in return as an earnest of her affections. Hemingway sometimes sent her his manuscripts and paid attention to what she said about them. "Since she knows about the things I write about which are people, country, life and death and problems of honor and of conduct, I value her opinion more than that of many critics," he said in a special eulogy of her which he wrote for *Life* magazine in 1952.

Dietrich's men friends usually came trailing their own myth: there are few photographs of her with personable but total strangers. And she tended to subsume something of the celebrity's status or outlook into the way she presented herself with him in public. Thus with Erich Maria Remarque she became noticeably more pessimistic and brooding. Remarque represented the warrior type (Generals Gavin and Patton would occupy this role, but as actual warriors, in a few years' time). Remarque, best known for *All Quiet on the Western Front*, an agonized but reflective account of war's wastefulness distilled from the author's World War I experiences on the German side, spoke directly to Dietrich's own upbringing in a "soldier's household." His theme would later be sentimentalized into Dietrich's famous song "Where Have All the Flowers Gone?" She in turn is said to have inspired the heroine of his postwar novel *Arc de Triomphe*.

Though Dietrich was said to "fall in and out of love like shelling peas," she stayed faithful to her men: her affairs survived the gossip columnists who linked their names; and such men, in turn, stayed friends with her long after they had ceased to be her companions. This, too, is in keeping with the romantic myth which does not need the actual presence of the beloved and frequently draws power and poignancy from his or her absence. But Dietrich's feelings never publicly transgressed the verifiable if not very conspicuous fact that she was a respectable married woman. Helpfully, filmgoers the world over largely forgot this, if they had ever known it. And not just filmgoers. Even Miklos Rosza recalled in his memoirs how puzzled he was to find himself being introduced to a woman who looked like Marlene Dietrich but was addressed as "Mrs. Sieber."

Towards such men friends, Dietrich showed the devotion of a nurse, mother and big sister rather than that of a lover. She had a passion for making men comfortable, consoling them in misfortune, doing all the things that men (then) were not supposed to be good at doing—like cooking the meals and overseeing domestic chores. "Inside every *femme fatale* is a *Hausfrau* struggling to get out," commented the London theater critic Milton Shulman. Time and again the recollections of celebrities who have become her friends testify to the fact that no sooner had she taken a liking to them than she was seized by a passion to cook for them, shower them with gifts, or have their horoscopes cast by her onetime astrologer Carroll Richter of California. She also dosed them liberally with medicines if they admitted to being off-color. She seemed to treat such men as if

Dietrich's friends in the 1930s were almost invariably celebrities. The roster included John Gilbert (*above, left*), and Douglas Fairbanks, Jr. (*above, right*, in London). Photographers found her dining in a Hollywood restaurant with Dolores Del Rio and her husband, the noted art director Cedric Gibbons (*right*), and at a famous Santa Monica Pier party with Carole Lombard, Cary Grant and Richard Barthelmess (*opposite: above, left*) where everyone was expected to come in "old clothes." Other well-known companions included the emigré film director Fritz Lang (*opposite: above, right*) and the British actor Ronald Colman (on his yacht, *opposite*).

Despite the succession of male friends, Dietrich remained a respectable married woman with a growing daughter and an occasionally visible husband (*left*). She was also the proud possessor of a substantial Beverly Hills home (*below*), where young Maria was reared as strictly as her mother had been in Kaiser Wilhelm's Berlin.

they were children. Cecil Beaton had surely a slight edge on his voice when he said, "I think above all that she's the schoolboys' delight." The English actor John Clements was playing a youthful second-lead in a prewar Dietrich film which required much open-air location work in wintertime. "I sat about turning slowly blue," he recalled. "After a while, [she] noticed my pitiful plight, whisked me into her car, which was on the lot, and forced a double brandy down my throat."

The tragedies other people suffered appealed powerfully to Dietrich's instinct for helping and healing. When she got to know John Gilbert in her early Hollywood days, this most romantic archetype (after Valentino) of the silent cinema was a fallen idol whose appeal had withered in the greater realism of the talkies. He had become a deeply self-destructive alcoholic whom even Garbo's charitable efforts—exerted in return for the favors he had done her at the start of her career—had failed to restore to popularity when she maneuvered him into the co-starring role opposite her in *Queen Christina*. Dietrich, in her turn, attempted to maneuver Gilbert into Lubitsch's production of *Desire*. But a premonitory heart attack ruined his chances—and he died within a day or so of Gary Cooper's being cast. Since the romantic hero was beyond her consolation, Dietrich went to the aid and comfort of his former wife, Leatrice Joy, and their child. At the sale of Gilbert's pitiful effects in August 1936, her agent bid up a pair of Gilbert's cotton bed-sheets to ten times what they were worth; and she followed up this *memento mori* by virtually "adopting" his eleven-year-old daughter and for many years acting as the child's unofficial godmother.

Dietrich's own strict upbringing in obedience repeated itself in the way she reared her own daughter. Before Maria saw a film, either one of her mother's or some other star's, it was previewed for suitability. "I shall permit her to see *The Garden of Allah*," Dietrich said, "but I keep her away from all stories of triangles and other situations." A Shirley Temple film was one which did not pass mother's inspection: she thought its story of a marital breakup, however temporary, was a vulgar thing in which to involve a child. Perhaps the all-wise Shirley was not looked on with favor as a role model for Maria, although mother seems to have been quite amused when her child mimicked glamorous stars of her mother's generation. "Do your imitation of Joan Crawford, Maria," a reporter on location with *The Garden of Allah* testified to hearing Dietrich ask. (A surprise: since interviews with Dietrich were invariably short on humor.) "The child . . . tilted her head sideways at an erotic angle, raising a languid hand to her face, brushing away an imaginary lock of hair, slowly turning full face towards the camera with exaggerated intensity in her eyes."[40]

When Dietrich agreed to make *Knight Without Armor* in England for Alexander Korda, in 1937, a reporter asked if this was done to prove to the world that Dietrich could still be Dietrich without Hollywood. He got a cool put-down: "There is no challenge in it. I simply feel that everyone should have a change of scenery." But she was already complaining, along with other stars, of the

Knight Without Armor, produced by Alexander Korda in his Denham Studios outside London, did not turn out to be one of Dietrich's triumphs, but it allowed her to bask for a while in the adulation of her British admirers. The film's director was Jacques Feyder, seen (*left*) coaching Marlene for the bathtub scene—a sequence omitted when the Korda production was first screened in America.

"excessive" taxes levied on the wealthy by the Roosevelt New Deal administration. "If America were my home, I would not object . . . but it is very discouraging to earn a large sum of money and yet have so little left."[41] England, with most of her expenses met by Korda's generosity, had its attractions; and Maria would learn to speak English properly. She took the precaution of entrusting herself to Jacques Feyder, yet another of those directors who had guided Garbo. And she had the romantic Robert Donat as her co-star (asthma permitting: such an affliction was characteristically treated by her with a nurse's understanding, not a star's irritation, during the days, lengthening into weeks, it kept him from filming). But *Knight Without Armor* is a poor film in every way, typical of the English studios' then underdeveloped scripts and lamentable lack of technical polish—the failure of its photography to match the continuity of individual shots is as distracting as a series of jump cuts. Its story was no worse than some she had been in: she played a Russian countess caught up in the 1917 Revolution, alternating between being a Bolshevik prisoner and the toast of the White Russians' officers' mess, and finally transported to safety on a hospital train, while Donat clings doggedly to the outside of the convalescent compartment for the 500-mile trip in midwinter. The scenes that might have exploited Dietrich's glamour and mystery are badly bungled. She is an all-too-solid presence in the impromptu foam bath that the romantically inclined White Russians have whipped up for her in their makeshift HQ, and her dialogue with an appreciative servant woman supervising her immersion in the tub is embarrassing because of ribald innuendo and crude miscasting. The well-oiled Hollywood production machine that guarded the stars as precious assets was simply not available to Feyder in the more casual hands-in-the-pocket world of Korda's Denham Studios. He utterly quenches Dietrich's allure by terminating a perfect Von Sternberg set-up of her sitting down to dinner with her Czarist rescuers just as the men are shaking out their table napkins.

Yet Dietrich took the same proprietorial interest in the film that she had shown in *The Garden of Allah*. She was paid a token penny by the British crew, then more in awe of a Hollywood star than would be the case today, whenever she contributed a suggestion for lighting or shooting a scene. She took particular pride in arranging "several angles for a scene between Mr. Donat and myself so that we would appear in the same shot simultaneously." Her thoroughness was confirmed by the strip of developed 35mm. film she carried around and showed to interviewers in order to prove her point. "You can direct here any time you want," Korda told her, after one "demonstration," before wandering off, as the reporter put it, "in his vague Hungarian manner." Dietrich set no high hopes on *Knight Without Armor* and was probably able to shrug off its lukewarm notices. Anyhow, the social life she led in London confirmed that, in the public mind, she was a star at the height of power, beauty and public favor.

She wore "Hollywood fashions," sometimes Travis Banton's creations, which made her stand out strikingly against the English scene. At one white-tie dinner hosted by Korda she entered wearing a black turban whose tail dangled exotically over one shoulder and a silver brocaded tunic, with a huge green semiprecious stone at the side of the collar, flaring dramatically out from her waist like a mini-crinoline over a straight black skirt down to the ground but slit to her calf, the better to display her legs. Douglas Fairbanks, Jr., often escorted her to theater first nights and to film premières. She urged Fairbanks to accept the role of Rupert of Henzau in *The Prisoner of Zenda*. Was she ambitious to play the part of Queen Flavia in this classic piece of arch-romanticism whose contagious gallantry might have been a welcome antidote to the wishy-washy heroics of *Knight Without Armor*? If so, she was to be disappointed: Selznick was not to use her again.

Crowds would often collect outside the Ritz waiting for her to emerge from lunch. At the London première of the MGM film *Romeo and Juliet*, it required the entire male staff of the cinema, supplemented by twenty stout hearts from the corps of commissionaires and fifty policemen, to hold back 5,000 people in the Haymarket who broke through the cordon, pulled off Dietrich's red-lace head shawl and were already pawing at her red-bordered black dress. She was saved from dishevelment by two of the ushers hoisting her on to their shoulders and carting her above the mob into the safety of the lobby. Next day, the *Daily Telegraph* even carried an apprehensive editorial on the affair. No wonder the Russian Revolution, as glimpsed in *Knight Without Armor*, felt tame: Dietrich vs. the People was nothing to the turmoil of the people worshipping Dietrich.

She was also written up endlessly in the gossip columns, which described her as "the only woman in London who dares wear a hat while dancing in a restaurant." Sometimes she was criticized for her "mysterious standoffishness," which the English put down to typical Teutonic arrogance: Von Ribbentrop was then Hitler's ambassador in London and "German" characteristics were not too popular. However, nothing could be better proof that Dietrich's name was popularly associated with Hollywood, not Hitler, than the crowds' applause. It was probably at this time that Ribbentrop made his attempt to woo her back to Germany with the news that the Führer wished to bestow on her their country's highest civilian decoration. Her reply was not encouraging: "Let him try." He did not; though he is believed to have sent her a compensatory Christmas tree.

Dietrich enjoyed herself in London. But it proved an unwise move to be away from Hollywood so long—and even less helpful, when she returned in the spring of 1937, not to bring home the goods in the shape of a box-office hit. Coincidentally, it was now that she took out application papers for American citizenship, though her husband, over in Paris, remained a German citizen, a fact which was to lead to his brief internment early in the war.

Her new film for Paramount, *Angel* (1937), preserved her image as a European woman of the world. This was wise, for Lubitsch, who directed it, knew his way round that part of the globe and guided her faultlessly through a story based—one almost writes, "of course"—on an old Hungarian stage success. Dietrich played the wife of an English diplomat (Herbert Marshall), but with a hint of her more exotic Russian past which still compels her to go off, by private plane, on secret weekends in Paris. There, with eyelids fluttering duplicitously, she signs herself into grand hotels as "Mrs. Brown." The nickname "Angel" is given her by the debonair American (Melvyn Douglas) who meets this mystery lady in a society bordello while she is visiting her old *patronne*. He turns out to be her husband's old wartime buddy. Dietrich is forever being mistaken for someone else: her past is always threateningly latent in her present. Lubitsch is in his element in this world where the servants share the snobberies of their betters and the power politics of Europe keep the diplomat husband from the marital enjoyment of his wife. "What's worrying you?" Dietrich asks, as an inconveniently timed telegram arrives in Marshall's bedroom from the League of Nations. "France?" "No, Yugoslavia." "Oh . . . Yugoslavia." Eventually, he learns to pay more attention to what his wife does than to what Yugoslavia is getting up to.

Dietrich, too, is in her element. It is true that, as Herman Weinberg observes, Lubitsch always emphasized Dietrich's feminine side: not for him the masculine ambiguities that Von Sternberg laminated into her female gender. But she, too, knows how to move round this world where husbands should always be a little uncertain of their wives, where a man's ability to order a delicious dinner confirms his success with women and where illicit love is implied by a sip from a champagne glass that seems to turn it into a communion cup.

Angel is arguably Dietrich's best prewar film outside the Von Sternberg cycle. But against the screwball comedy genre then in vogue in Hollywood, it looked decidedly un-American. It was meant to be, of course, though this did not save it from critics who generally found it too slight, too dated, too self-conscious. "Clearly Mr. Lubitsch's *Angel* is among the fallen," wrote Frank S. Nugent in the *New York Times*, adding: "Miss Dietrich is at the root of its evils. She is still a lovely lady, glamorously gowned, but she has the unhappy gift of absorbing the camera's attention to the exclusion . . . of the narrative itself. . . . The character is too shallow to hold the destinies of two intelligent men."[42] One feels tempted to say, "Really? Who are these men?" But this opinion, which others shared, reflected the impasse which Dietrich had reached. She had been stranded by changing fashion. It was appropriate that an additional half-inch had been added by the makeup man to the length of her eyelids—her career had reached the same point of artificial elongation.

To be fair, most of Hollywood's leading ladies who had made a successful transition from the silents to the talkies in 1929–30 were running into the same sort of trouble as they tried to keep their welcome at the box office. The studios, sensing this from the dwindling receipts, had embarked on the last great prewar buying in of European talents. A second generation of non-American actresses— Hedy Lamarr, Greer Garson, Ilona Massey, Ingrid Bergman—were being recruited by the studio heads to supplement the likes of Garbo, Crawford or Dietrich who were too familiar or simply too old to play younger leads. The exhibitors' disenchantment was made brutally plain. A trade paper—significantly

ADOLPH ZUKOR PRESENTS

MARLENE DIETRICH

"ANGEL"

WITH

HERBERT MARSHALL
MELVYN DOUGLAS

EDWARD EVERETT HORTON · ERNEST COSSART
LAURA HOPE CREWS · HERBERT MUNDIN

PRODUCED AND DIRECTED BY

ERNST LUBITSCH

one serving owners of independent theaters, not the big circuits which were still owned by the same companies that ran the studios supplying them with films—published a notorious red-bordered advertisement labeling Dietrich as box-office poison. If so, she was not the only toxic talent: others so labeled included Garbo, Crawford, Hepburn and Astaire. (True to how these things go, all were to have enormous and unexpected box-office successes within a year or so.)

Dietrich and Paramount had separated; and for the next year she was like a glamorously displaced character from a Lubitsch film, drifting around Europe, comfortably enough, with no visible means of support, checking into grand hotels (though always under her own name) and seeing many man whose *savoir-vivre* matched her own—Boyer, Gabin, Remarque among them. She ran into James Joyce at Fouquet's. "I saw you in *The Blue Angel*," he said, confirming how the leading experimental writer of his day could be as banal as any film fan. "Then, *monsieur*, you saw the best of me," Dietrich replied. It is what one *hopes* screen goddesses say, particularly those who have been toppled off their columns and have picked themselves up with dignity and restraint.

But it must also be recorded that after the war, when Dietrich was again in Paris and ran into another *habitué* of good eating places, the critic and film historian Thomas Quinn Curtiss, she told a different story. "*The Blue Angel* made and ruined me," she said, relating how she had been set to play Gretchen in *Faust* when Von Sternberg made his offer—and ever after she was obliged to play the high-priced courtesan. Perhaps—and then again, perhaps not. Stars are notorious for telling admirers what they wish to hear.

Dietrich became an American citizen in the second week of June 1939, an act which her new government ungraciously acknowledged by claiming $284,000 in back taxes. Even more inconveniently, the Internal Revenue men demanded it just as she was boarding the liner *Normandie* in New York, along with Sieber and Maria. Lubitsch might have put his maliciously comic touch on the pierside scene as officials haggled over whether or not to allow her thirty-six pieces of luggage to sail with her and perspiring porters kept heaving them on and off the ship.

The brisk dialogue between Dietrich and the Revenue men usefully establishes a rough scale of remuneration for her services at this time. She declared that in 1936 and 1937 she had paid just over $100,000 in yearly taxes—"I didn't work in 1938, so I can't imagine why they are holding my things." Not so, came the stony-hearted answer: she had worked for Korda and owed $284,000—a claim reflecting the enhanced fee which Korda had had to pay for the services of a star who he hoped would assist in selling his film to the American market.

When the tax officials threatened to detain Sieber, and the *Normandie* had already been delayed ninety minutes, Dietrich surrendered to the necessity of the moment and left her diamonds and a famous emerald collection as collateral. She was in a hurry, concerned about her mother and sister in Germany and hoping to persuade them to leave that country before the rumors of war turned into a fact. Either they were obstinate or she was too late. Already Julius Streicher's vicious

Back in Hollywood, Dietrich made her last film under contract to Paramount, *Angel*, in which she plays a woman-with-a-past caught up between the affections of her husband, Herbert Marshall, and a would-be-lover, Melvyn Douglas (*above, right*). The director was Ernst Lubitsch, pictured on the set with his usual cigar in hand.

Making glamorous portraits of the stars was a major Hollywood preoccupation. E. R. Richee, a master of the genre, is shown (with stylist John Engstead, seated) setting up a Dietrich session in 1936 (*opposite*). One of the results is seen in the inset. Soon, a second generation of European leading ladies began to arrive in Hollywood. Pictured here are (*clockwise from above*) Greer Garson, Hedy Lamarr and Ingrid Bergman.

In the days of shipboard crossings, actresses did not travel light. When Dietrich was about to sail for Europe in 1939, Internal Revenue officials threatened to impound thirty-six pieces of her luggage for nonpayment of income taxes. Just before that, the German-born actress had been sworn in as a U.S. citizen (*above*), wearing a wide-brimmed fedora from one of her several Lily Daché hatboxes.

newspaper, *Der Stürmer*, had branded her a "traitress" for taking out American citizenship. She did not cross the German frontier, but tried to exert influence on her family from Paris, though without effect. While there, she confirmed on which side her loyalties lay by appearing on an open truck in the Place de l'Opéra on July 14, France's national day, singing her *Blue Angel* numbers and then descending into the crowds and dancing with a Foreign Legionnaire: it was as if Lola-Lola had met Gary Cooper.

During the last few weeks of European peace she was vacationing at the Hotel du Cap, Eden Roc, along with Raimu, Gabin and Von Sternberg, when she received a film proposal that was to restore her fortunes dramatically. It came from a man in every way the opposite of her first mentor.

Joe Pasternak was a European-born entrepreneur who had learned how to wheel and deal, survive and (occasionally) thrive in Hollywood. Where Von Sternberg nurtured obsessions, Pasternak created opportunities. He had a commercial sense of where popular taste was at, and enough artistic calculation to enable him to get on with people of talent and temperament. In his time, he had been a waiter and thus knew how to make people think they wanted what he wished to give them. A small-town boy from the almost unpronounceable village of Szilagy-Smolno in an almost unlocatable area of Transylvania, he had a cocksureness about the wider world; he was by nature a risk taker. He gambled on unknown quantities, on unexpected proposals, on unconsidered ideas which had maybe just occurred to him and thus lost none of their vitality in the telling and selling.

Pasternak had met Dietrich before she left for Hollywood in 1930. He had been producing a long-forgotten historical "epic" at Neubabelberg Studios on a set adjacent to that of *The Blue Angel*, and with Von Sternberg's slightly chilly permission had introduced himself to Dietrich in her dressing room. As he recalled in his memoirs, "she was wreathed coolly in a sheer peignoir and nothing else, shimmering like the moon on a cloudy night." (Pasternak, one can see, was a poet, at least in the limited application of the word to the rhymes that songwriters find for the ends of lines.) He had even tried to get Universal to make an offer for Dietrich, and although Carl Laemmle indicated no interest—he had enough Germans at Universal—this interest may well have caused Paramount to clinch their deal with self-protective speed.

One of Pasternak's German chores had been spotting European movies that could be remade in Hollywood as American subjects. This was quite a minor industry in the 1930s. Lubitsch had remade Brigitte Helm's *The Wonderful World of Angoulême* as *Desire*; a film called *Kleine Mutter* starring Franciska Gaal became *Bachelor Mother* starring Ginger Rogers; even *Top Hat* owed its origins to an obscure European movie. When he began producing his own films in Hollywood, Pasternak continued this technique—he took great European talents and both Americanized and popularized them. "There is no artist who does not wish to enlarge his audience," was his shibboleth. Simple: but it worked. He

Dietrich's first film as an American citizen turned out to be a Western, *Destry Rides Again*, which thoroughly changed her image. The idea came from the producer Joe Pasternak, shown (standing, *above*) with the star and the film's director, George Marshall, in Universal's canteen during a break in the shooting.

persuaded Lauritz Melchior, the great Wagnerian heldentenor and star of the Met, to appear in a film called *The Thrill of Romance*, singing all-American ditties. He persuaded José Iturbi, the distinguished concert pianist, to play boogie-woogie for a Judy Garland picture. He gave Deanna Durbin's likable homespun personality a light cultural dressing of popular classics in *Three Smart Girls* and then had Stokowski and a full symphony orchestra follow her around in *One Hundred Men and a Girl*. It was in this mood, riding high on Deanna Durbin's success, that he now proposed to Dietrich, the world-weary European sophisticate, that she do—a Hollywood Western.

The idea was shrewder than it first sounded. A Western saloon bar in the 1880s had plenty in common with a Berlin cabaret in the 1920s: a brash, bawdy milieu, an exuberantly bullying madam figure able to meet the other sex on its own terms, gusto with a taunting undertone to it, a vigorous insistence on making one's own rules and breaking conventional standards—with all of which Dietrich was perfectly familiar from her own early days as a Berlin soubrette. Maybe she had refined her origins out of all recognition: but she had never abandoned them. Pasternak knew that Universal owned the remake rights of Tom Mix's 1932 Western *Destry Rides Again*, about an able-bodied loner who uses fists and guns to tame an uppity township. The feminine interest of the original film had little to do but stand around the saloon and wait for her man to come home, dead or alive. Pasternak reversed the usual sex roles on which the genre depended. He also switched the images by which the stars were customarily recognized. Thus James Stewart, usually the likably callow boy-next-door, became Destry's son, a pacifist who doesn't believe in settling disputes by force, but stands passively by until his vestigial manhood is roused despite himself. Dietrich inherited all the film's masculine qualities. Instead of simperingly entreating her man to look after himself, she puts up her own fists and tells the roughneck *habitués* where to get off—or get out. It was the sort of cynical reversal of expectations that Brecht might have hit on, had he and Hollywood been able to like each other better.

Dietrich agreed to do the film, despite Universal's cutting her fee to $75,000, only a sixth of what she had been used to earning. (The money, it was said, paid for the bribes and the fares to secure the safe passage of German friends and refugees from the Fatherland, which was to be at war within a week.) Coincidentally or not, her husband, soon released from internment by the French, found a job in Universal's foreign department in Hollywood before his chicken farm was bought for him.

Destry Rides Again (1939) probably employed more old German hands than any other celebration of the Old West. Pasternak employed an ex-UFA *protégé*, Felix Joachimsohn (soon to be "Jackson"), to write the script and enlisted Frederick (formerly Friedrich) Hollander and Frank Loesser to give Dietrich back the growling "German sound" in that cynical ballad which goes, "See what the boys in the back room will have/And give them the poison they name,/See what the boys in the back room will have/And tell them I died of the same." It made Dietrich the toast of a male-oriented world in which she played Frenchy, queen of the Last Chance Saloon, a woman who was one of the boys, and whose come-hither invitation was countermanded by a keep-your-distance self-possession. Her face was coarsened, too, by lowering her penciled-in eyebrows, rouging her cheekbones and giving her fuller lips. The setting completed the thorough Americanization of Marlene Dietrich.

Lest exhibitors pale at the thought of a heroine with more guts than the nominal male star, the script took care in the last few minutes to turn Dietrich into the self-sacrificing woman who dies while saving her man from the villain's bullet: the sort of "unconditional love" that American filmgoers demanded and that she was temperamentally inclined to give. But as well as shedding her air of mystery and her European mannerisms, Dietrich also jettisoned something even more inhibiting to box-office success in America—her dignity. She has nothing perverse about her now. Instead of planting an ambiguous kiss on the lips of a virginal girl, as she had done in *Morocco*, she is now the one who gets slapped by the customers—playfully and on the backside. Her singing voice has no mocking innuendo: it startles, instead, as it plumbs a beery, down-to-earth baritone. A lucky rabbit's paw snared in her frilly madam's garter brings those once divine

Destry's most memorable moment comes when the town sheriff (James Stewart) dumps a bucket of water over Dietrich and her brawling adversary (Una Merkel). Marlene is momentarily stunned but quickly grabs a gun and ends triumphant.

legs of hers down to the level of the barroom floor. She also emphasizes a very American part of her anatomy, whose existence had hitherto been hardly suspected, when she drops a few silver dollars down her cleavage. This uninhibited gesture was supposed to elicit a cry from a grizzled prospector of "There's gold in them thar hills." But Hollywood censorship would have none of *that*! So Pasternak substituted the quip, "I'd rather have money in the bank."

Instead of reducing her men to erotic degradation in the European manner of such things, the only humiliation she inflicts on anyone is to wager $30 against Mischa Auer's pants—and collects. And now with total disregard for the looks she once used to double-check in a cheval glass positioned beside the camera, she engaged Una Merkel in an Amazonian rough-and-tumble on the barroom floor, both of them tearing hair-dos and costumes to shreds until they are finally separated like spitting cats by a pail of cold water from James Stewart, whereupon, dripping but otherwise unquenched, she expels him from the saloon in a hail of bottles, squelches up to the bar and musters the admiring townsfolk with a cry of "Who'll buy me a drink?" Ernest Hemingway might have contributed the additional dialogue. Lola-Lola, though, would have looked at the new Dietrich and perhaps thought the floozy brash.

Destry Rides Again deserved its huge success. But, unfortunately, success of this magnitude—even for those who enjoy it—can be as dangerous as failure. For if the film changed Dietrich's image from that of an impeccably dressed sophisticate or a mysteriously shadowed *femme fatale* into a full-blooded woman who made the advances and fought for the prize with tooth and claw, then filmmakers drew the conclusion that this was how she should be—and how she should stay. And stay this way she did in film after film.

Pasternak also produced her next Universal picture and showed how ruthlessly he was prepared to standardize the *Destry Rides Again* formula. *Seven Sinners* (1940) was a broad burlesque of the Sadie Thompson genre—"just a little broader," Bosley Crowther wrote, "[and] Mae West would be in the shade." In other words, it was *Destry Rides Again* relocated in the South Seas, matelots replacing cowpunchers in the saloon where Bijou the torch singer is now the star turn. Her male sidekicks are the same as before: one dumb but lovable bruiser (Broderick Crawford); one comic courtier (Mischa Auer as magician-cum-pickpocket); one standard-issue leading man (John Wayne, torn between love and the Navy), and a repertoire of songs sung to an exuberant male audience who are both tamed by her and roused to competitive fisticuffs among themselves, thus dismantling the joint—their way of paying respects to its queen. There is also a lightly ambiguous mixture of genders, in this case Dietrich in tailored ensign's whites and gold-braided cap (still an officer, we observe) singing "The Man's in the Navy" (by Hollander and Loesser).

The film has one example of how time has altered custom: when she sings "We've been in love before/Haven't we all?" from her berth among the rough company traveling steerage, it is now the pretty girl on the top deck who tosses

Frenchy, queen of the Last Chance Saloon in *Destry Rides Again*. The erstwhile European woman of mystery had metamorphosed into a down-to-earth hoyden.

A moment of reflection during the production of *Pittsburgh* (*opposite*). "It is around this time that one feels Dietrich's own interest in her film career slackening."

A trio of Dietrich vehicles from the early 1940s. She played a European adventuress in *The Flame of New Orleans* (with Bruce Cabot, *above*), a gin-palace queen in *The Spoilers* (with Randolph Scott and John Wayne, *right*) and a clip-joint hostess in *Manpower* (below).

1270-P9

her the emblematic kiss in the shape of an unappreciated coin. The lesson that it's a man's world notwithstanding what the women in it do to the men is literally punched home by Broderick Crawford in order to teach Dietrich the rough lesson that Wayne's destiny is to stay with his first love, the Navy, and not be seduced on to the rocks by this South Seas Circe. The fight, though, is only a pale reprise of *Destry*'s.

With a couple of exceptions, Dietrich's next films simply proved that she had once again landed in a rut. In short order, she was a European adventuress (*The Flame of New Orleans*: 1941), a clip-joint hostess (*Manpower*: 1941), a gin-palace queen (*The Spoilers*: 1942) and a kept woman (*Pittsburgh*: 1942). Even René Clair, whom Pasternak signed up the minute the Frenchman arrived for wartime exile, could not do *much* with a dual-role period comedy resembling *Angel* in everything but wit and cynicism (*The Flame of New Orleans*). One scene, though, wears the Lubitsch touch: it features the newly engaged Dietrich singing an atypical ballad of spring like innocence at the piano while an ex-lover passes the (unheard) tales of her scarlet past among the assembled future in-laws and her prospective husband. Little else shows this piquancy. Dietrich might have done better working more often for independent producers, less hidebound by studio formulae, for Charles Feldman's production of *The Lady Is Willing* (1942) gave her a welcome change of pace: a light comedy role (in a plausible setting) as a Broadway star who decides to raise an abandoned baby, which she treats as a girl until she discovers differently. Mitchell Leisen, the director, has left a record of the lengths Dietrich went to in order to play it realistically: "She could cry hysterically on cue, but she didn't think that was enough . . . so she sprayed a horrible fluid into her eyes until they were all red and puffed up, and then she really let go and sobbed."[43]

It is around this time that one feels Dietrich's own interest in her film career slackening again. The war in Europe was slowly changing her life and would soon immeasurably expand her world. Hollywood must have seemed a very small place to someone so *engagé* by the distant conflict. She was in her early forties, by no means old, yet too old in Hollywood terms to obtain leading roles with ease. Her private life showed the signs of restiveness. Close friendships were severed by the war: Jean Gabin, even more fractious than she in his Hollywood exile, felt patriotic stirrings and went to North Africa to join the Free French. She began recording her songs, in the languages of both the Allies and the enemy, for broadcasting overseas by the Voice of America. She was in fact being reshaped by circumstances and her own will for the new role she was destined to play: the role of international entertainer. She was drawing closer to the experience that had shaped her outlook, her loyalties, her preferences in love and her very special sympathy for the life that defines itself in valor. The war that Dietrich went to now was both a fulfillment of her past and a rehearsal for her future.

ON THE
WORLD
STAGE

ON THE WORLD STAGE

It is not generally known that Metro-Goldwyn-Mayer helped finance Marlene Dietrich's war effort—from the fee paid for a film that she never made for that studio. The MGM archives in Culver City, probably the best preserved in Hollywood, reveal the details of a transaction that caused embarrassment at the studio for the better part of ten years—and ultimately a write-off of $50,000. That money, one presumes, contributed to Dietrich's fulfilling the intention she had in mind when interviewed in the *Los Angeles Times* in November 1943: "I want to go abroad and do what I can for the boys." She traveled on MGM's money.

Dietrich had already donated her patriotic jot to the war effort by appearing, as herself, in a morale-boosting all-star movie entitled *Follow the Boys* (released in 1944) in which she was sawn in half by two GIs under Orson Welles's instructions. Meanwhile, on October 26, 1943, she signed an MGM contract for two movies—at $100,000 *for both*. This was a considerable drop from her usual fee, even though her name on the billing of what was to be the first film, *Kismet* (1944), compensated her with ninety percent size of type against Ronald Colman's hundred-percent supremacy. *Kismet* was in the genre of Ali Baba-esque escapism, the nature of which is amply conveyed just by the description of what Dietrich wore as Jamilla, queen of the Grand Vizier's harem in Old Baghdad. (The word "harem," according to the MGM papers, had to be struck out of the scenario early on due to censorial squeamishness from the Hays Office.) Her arms and breasts were covered with bangles attached to some sheer skin-toned material; her fingernails were painted carmine and her legs encrusted with four coats of gold "paint"; while hair stylist Sydney Guilaroff constructed a four-inch-high topknot with black chiffon veiling attached. With this "extension," and wearing high heels, she stood nearly six feet tall. The Hays Office decreed that her navel must not be visible under the swathe of chiffon, but that a "pantie line" *must* show under her harem trousers in case filmgoers were to get the idea that she was naked.

It was the first time Dietrich had had to perform a "novelty dance" in a film: it has to be admitted that, like Garbo's temple dance in *Mata Hari*, her movements are "fabricated" for her in the editing of the film rather than "performed" by her, since she seems to use a clever series of artistic "poses" interrupted by shrewd cutaway shots to give the adequate impression of a sensuous court entertainment. But in case one thinks she took things easy and left the heavy work to her dance

Follow the Boys was an all-star wartime extravaganza meant to boost the morale of soldiers and civilians alike. Dietrich appeared as the accomplice of magician Orson Welles.

tutor, Jack Cole, the MGM archives record that on October 29, 1943, "because of bruises received by her while doing a dance number in *Kismet* on October 26, the actress was unable to render services on October 27, 28 and today."

Kismet completed shooting on the last day of 1943—and Dietrich, despite collecting her fee, never returned to MGM to make the second film due under her contract. The MGM files show increasing concern about this, and for the next seven years the lawyers and studio executives exchanged memoranda about Dietrich's present whereabouts as well as speculation about her likely intentions. It really was not her fault, though. Part of the trouble seems to have been that MGM could find no subject suitable for her: they had to have one ready to go into production at the same time as they served notice on her to report to their Culver City studio, since the contemplated picture would have an estimated twelve-week shooting schedule. (If Dietrich hung about *after* reporting, with no picture ready to start, that would involve MGM in agreed "overage" payments of a massive $10,000 a week!) So the years passed until, under California law, the seven-year statute of limitations freed Marlene Dietrich from the obligation of earning the rest of the $100,000 already paid her.

On April 3, 1944, MGM received an inquiry from the Army Intelligence Division: it concerned "the loyalty, integrity and discretion" of one Maria Sieber (also known as Marlene Dietrich). Louis K. Sidney, the studio's assistant treasurer, replied in satisfying terms: "To our knowledge, she has never been connected with any subversive groups." He generously gave her age (then forty-two) as "approximately thirty-nine."

Dietrich had for months been imploring highly placed friends at the USO (United Services Organization) to send her abroad on more active assignments than simply selling War Bonds round the United States. In April 1944 she got her wish—and embarked on the experiences that shaped and annealed the final Dietrich. It was probably at this time, in the dramatic circumstances of World War II, that she sensed she was not only a legend, but a legend independent of any particular picture or publicity buildup. She could now stand on the secure platform of her own myth. Stardom is rich in such moments of mythic recognition—like Chaplin's traveling the breadth of the USA on what he thought would be a normal train journey in 1914 and discovering, from the gathering crowds at the wayside halts and the jammed streets outside the New York terminal, that he was "big"; bigger even than he'd believed himself to be back in Hollywood.

Dietrich, wearing the honorary rank of colonel, took off with a USO party of three other entertainers bound for North Africa via fueling stops in Greenland and the Azores. She did her first show at the Algiers opera house, singing songs from her films, performing a mind-reading act taught her by Orson Welles, and then—with her musical saw—playing plaintive, haunting and what, in such circumstances (she was a lone woman surrounded by 5,000 GIs), seemed sensual music on the curious instrument. It was in this highly charged arena that the

Dietrich's last movie before going overseas to entertain the troops was *Kismet*, which opened on Broadway (*above*) in 1944. Dietrich was billed below the title for the first time in her U.S. career. Photos taken in the studio during its shooting the previous year show the star being coached by her dance tutor, Jack Cole, and inspecting her gilded legs.

Wearing the uniform of a WAAC and a pair of sensible walking shoes, Dietrich is seen strolling down a London street (*opposite, left*) in September 1944. Earlier that year she had visited the Italian front, where a photographer found her comparing "short snorters" (autographed banknotes) with Irving Berlin at a Fifth Army base (*opposite, below*). Wherever Dietrich went, she hobnobbed with the enlisted men and, on VE Day in Germany, shared a moment of elation with an impetuous GI (*left*).

image she had so often projected on the screen, of the woman who is at one with the fighting men, at last became flesh—and a part of daily reality, not fantasy.

In the repertoire she quickly elaborated (the musical saw was soon dropped), her relationship to servicemen—the audiences sometimes numbered 20,000, the men often coming to hear her sing with battlefield mud still caking flesh and uniform—was refined into a mood of comradeship and devotion. A shared hardship became for Dietrich a pledged brotherhood. It was a closer, more emotionally heightened pledge than any film audience could give her: this audience was immediate, virtually all-male and the embodiment of her own deep loyalties. The soldiers were too young ever to have experienced her phenomenal Hollywood debut or to remember her early films, which were not then commonplace fare on late-night television. If she could play upon their sentiments, then she could move audiences anywhere in the world.

On her return to New York, she recounted her experiences during a marathon fourteen-hour interview with Leo Lerman in one of his earliest contributions to *Vogue*. She recounted with relish the order she received that instead of her customary thirty-six pieces of luggage, she would have to rely on a frugal fifty-five pounds. Even so, Irene, the Hollywood couturière, designed four amazing evening gowns so heavily encrusted with sequins that they were virtual carapaces of glittering lights and reflected the beams from flashlights that her soldier-boy fans obligingly turned on to her when the local power supply failed. (Being composed almost entirely of sequins, they did not wrinkle and needed no ironing—the practical touch usually found somewhere in Dietrich's extravagances.)

She recalled the bunches of roses and heavily perfumed bougainvillea blossoms that GIs strung across her tent in welcoming garlands; the gin and tonics (more lemon slices than gin) they offered her before the show; the steak-and-onion cookouts on camp-fire braziers; the hospital visits, on which she would remake the rumpled beds of wounded men; the cow she milked to give nourishment to child refugees; the scarf that an Italian urchin begged off her (which she later saw he rented out to GIs to put under their bunkhouse pillows); the youngsters who held out autograph books and begged her signature for their mothers and fathers; the announcement she was privileged to make of the Normandy invasion on June 6, 1944, which stopped her act in a service camp in Italy and brought thousands of Allied men to their feet with cheer upon cheer; the lonely moonlight landing in liberated Paris; and the field hospitals where they would always ask first for "See What the Boys in the Back Room Will Have" ("When I'd sing," she told Lerman, "they'd swoon and scream the way bobbysoxers did at Sinatra"). Occasionally, some of the American and Allied casualties would tell her of injured German prisoners in the same hospital. "I'd go to these young, bland-faced Nazis and they'd ask me with tears in their eyes, 'Are you the *real* Marlene Dietrich?' All was forgotten, and I'd sing 'Lili Marlene' to everyone in that hospital. There was no greater moment in my life."[44]

Dressed in GI trousers and tan battle shirt, which she wore with the sleeves rolled up a workmanlike distance above the elbow, she followed the Fifth Army up the Italian peninsula in her jeep. Along the route were planted not only the usual direction posts, but signs reading "Dietrich Here Today" so that passing soldiers could drop in and catch the show. "When we were moving in convoy," she told Lerman, "boys passing by didn't know me. I always waved to the fellows. They'd shout back at me in Italian. They weren't used to seeing any other girls so far front. I'd yell back, kidding with them. And they'd shout, 'An American!' Someone would say, 'It's Dietrich.' Another would say, 'Aw, no!' There'd be an argument, and as the convoy would start off I'd discreetly show a leg. After that, they never seemed to have a doubt."

She spent more time with the ordinary GIs than with their commanders, but when she got to liberated Paris, General Patton made her his *protégée*, assigning her two bodyguards. Patton, the commander of the Third Army, and Dietrich admired each other's fearlessness, even recklessness. He sent her to entertain front-line battle stations and presented her with a pearl-handled pistol, the same as his own showy hand weaponry. Another American general, the youthful and dashing James Gavin, of the 88th Airborne Division, personally delivered her from the imminent threat of encirclement by the Germans during the last-gasp Battle of the Bulge in the Ardennes, by parachuting along with his men to where Dietrich and U.S. Army units were anxiously awaiting relief, and driving her to a safe area. Gallantry of a less buccaneering kind was displayed by an unlikely *chevalier*, Alexander Fleming, discoverer of penicillin. His antibiotic cured a dangerous pneumonia virus she contracted in Bari in 1944. Her thanksgiving gesture to him was the present of his horoscope—one hopes it registered such fateful intervention by the microbiologist—and she arranged for a basket of eggs to be sent to supplement Fleming's meager wartime rations. They continued on friendly terms—and so did the supply of eggs—up to Fleming's death in 1955.

She visited Belsen and its concentration camp and arranged medical care for her sister, who had been put in detention, along with other VIPs, in an apartment block near, though not actually in, the camp. Her mother was located about a month after the war ended, living in what had become the American sector of Berlin; she was to die shortly afterwards, even her resilient constitution weakened by the war's privations. Dietrich saw her parent into her grave, surrounded by the ruins of the stricken city.

Her return to Germany was an exceptionally emotional experience. It had been fifteen years since she had taken the liner *Bremen* to her new life in America. Now in her semi-military garb, or a Red Cross uniform, those famous million-dollar legs swathed against the cold in GI long johns, she looked around at the devastation and commented, "I guess that Germany deserves everything that's coming to her." There was always a small, grudging section of German public opinion that held—or was alleged by the papers to hold—this remark against her. For never at any time did Dietrich separate the ordinary Germans' responsibility for the human catastrophe they had brought upon themselves from the folly of the leaders they had elected and served. Dietrich had no half-loyalties.

Questioned by war correspondents about her film career, she was equally forthright. "I'm through with Hollywood—for ever. After doing nothing but entertain troops for fourteen months, I could never go back to that place." But patriotism, no more than love, scarcely pays the rent. Gradually, driven by her compulsion to work as much as her need for money, she yielded to the projects offered her.

It was more difficult than ever, though, to find a role to fit a woman who had outgrown the reach-me-down vehicles of Hollywood. A *crime passionnel* film, *Martin Roumagnac* (1946), made in France with Jean Gabin, fell flat wherever it was shown. Dietrich was not ideally cast as an Australian (this to account for her slightly "off" French accent); a putative German ancestry might have been more plausible, but would have been imprudent to adopt at this moment. She was still less acceptable as the owner of a pet shop in a provincial French town who falls for the earthy local builder. *Golden Earrings* (1948), her first postwar American picture, may have had aspirations to be part of the neo-realist trend that was now revolutionizing the looks of heroines in the Italian cinema: if so, they were not fulfilled by confining Dietrich's glamour to the raggle-taggle existence of a Hungarian gypsy wench with matted hair, greasy face, wind-tanned complexion and as little of her legs in view as possible. Her gypsy appearance went no deeper than the skin of a palmist's hand.

If she felt that Hollywood's machinery had seized up as far as she was concerned, she found compensation in a most unexpected role of—it might be said—her own creation. At the age of forty-seven, she became a grandmother. Her daughter Maria, after one short-lived marriage, had settled down happily with her second husband, William Riva, a designer of theater sets and playthings, and a son was born in 1948. To a star like Dietrich with so heavy an investment in *not* looking her age, the title of "The World's Most Glamorous Grandmother" was a mixed blessing, first borne with pride, then fortitude, then weariness, then indifference ("I'm sure that many women, younger than I am, are grandmothers") and then with unconcealed irritability that sprang from offended logic rather than piqued vanity. Yet the disjuncture between grandmotherly status and unfading (for the moment) beauty added a genuine dimension of fascination to Dietrich's appearances on screen and in public. As she grew older without actually looking her age before a camera or an audience, the effect became rather unearthly. Her grandson's birth was useful in reminding the postwar world that she had an off-screen life which was as normal, in the basic sense of producing offspring, as that of millions of women: yet her looks were strong enough still to keep thoughts of Grandma Moses out of the picture.

It was a surprise to find Dietrich in her next film, Billy Wilder's *A Foreign Affair* (1948), playing—of all things for her!—the ex-mistress of a former high-ranking Nazi reduced to earning her living as a café singer for the American

Remaining in Europe for a time, Dietrich made a French film entitled *Martin Roumagnac* with her friend Jean Gabin (*below*). Then it was back to Hollywood for *Golden Earrings* (above), in which she played a rather unconvincing Hungarian gypsy.

Three generations of Marlene's family. She is shown being met by her mother at Tempelhof Airport, Berlin, in September 1945 (*left*) and with her daughter in October 1951 (*above*).

Occupation forces and living "like a gorgeous booby trap" in the ruins of Berlin, where Wilder shot some of the film. At first she refused the role on obvious grounds, but after Wilder showed her a test he had made with June Havoc in the part, her objections weakened. Nothing changes a player's mind, perhaps, so much as another player's likely success. One clever-cynical line of dialogue provides the character of Erika von Schlütow with a sort of free pardon for past mistakes (and Dietrich with a conscience-salving *nihil obstat*): "Politics? Women pick out what's in fashion and change it like a spring hat. Everything is forgiven the eternal female." Or, rather, the eternal whore, the character whom Wilder once declared was the only one he found interesting in films.

A Foreign Affair, strafed at the time by indignant fire from critics, both lay and journalistic, for its "tastelessness" in portraying occupied Berlin as a black marketeer's paradise where the U.S. Army lubriciously invites its own corruption, has stood the test of time and even improved in truthfulness in an increasingly cynical world. Dietrich's Central European siren, whose dexterity at suviving is surely what commanded Wilder's sympathies, seduces in all but the fleshly sense Jean Arthur's virginal Congresswoman traveling on a fact-finding mission to Berlin. She is no Blue Angel this time, but a female Mephisto so slippery that when she gets her token comeuppance at the end, she needs five soldiers to march her off and keep an eye on her—and each other—lest she subvert them. She awakes the femininity in the almost genderless Congresswoman: but she teaches her a more lasting lesson than one to do with makeup and off-the-shoulder gowns. She makes her into a compromised woman. "Now you're one of us," she tells Jean Arthur—the American mouse caught in the trap of European depravity. Thus although Dietrich's role is given second billing, it is her ethos which permeates the picture and gives it its flavor. To create the authentic sound of moral decadence, Wilder enlisted Frederick Hollander. He wrote three new songs for Dietrich, "Ruins of Berlin," "Illusions" and the taunting "Black Market," which Erika von Schlütow sings in her nightclub with Hollander himself as accompanist. It was a nostalgic return to Berlin for the talents which had caught the tone of the times in that other nightclub, the Blue Angel, some twenty years earlier.

But such a film role was a rarity for Dietrich: there were only small pickings to be obtained from films over the next four years. She literally walked through a single scene (as herself) in *Jigsaw* (1949); a Dior wardrobe and a Cole Porter song, "The Laziest Girl in Town," also cut to her bias on classic lines, were the best things in Hitchcock's dishonest whodunit *Stage Fright* (1950); and in *No Highway in the Sky* (1951) she played an airborne movie star much like Marlene Dietrich. Save for Fritz Lang's *Rancho Notorious* (1952), which is only an echo of *Destry Rides Again*, Dietrich was employed as a Presence, rather than a performer. Her deadpan mask hid the boredom she was feeling: she threw any energies she could muster into overseeing her "presentation"—sometimes awakening the resentment of her autocratic directors. "Miss Dietrich is a professional," said

A Foreign Affair evoked strong memories of *The Blue Angel*. Dietrich was back in a Berlin cabaret, with Friedrich Holländer (now Frederick Hollander) again at the piano (*opposite*). The off-set photos show her singing to a playback (*left*) and in conversation with director Billy Wilder (*below*).

Hitchcock, like someone writing a politely deadly reference for an employee who possessed a high nuisance value. "A professional actress, a professional dress designer, a professional cameraman."[45]

And Fritz Lang complained that although her role as Altar Keane, an older sort of Frenchy, in *Rancho Notorious* had been written for her, Dietrich "resented going gracefully into that little tiny bit older category: she became younger and younger, until finally it was hopeless. . . . By the end of the picture, we didn't speak to each other any more."[46]

It is obvious what was happening. Once you have caught and held the attention of fighting men who may be literally about to die on the morrow, it is tedious to play a part for the professional purposes of movie people who are merely about to break for lunch. Dietrich hankered after the solo role she had played in the theater of war. She wanted to regain the total command of herself and her act that she had won as a hard-travelin' battlefront entertainer. She wanted to play upon the emotions of real live people, eliciting from them the male and the female and the in-between responses, so that every show would be a production number projecting the self-protective illusion of agelessness. In short, she wanted to be entirely of her own making. The goddess wanted to set herself in motion.

But there was another, more basic reason for the third transfiguration of Marlene Dietrich. As her fee for appearing in films had dropped, the one offered to her for appearing as herself in concert or cabaret had risen. "They worked on me for two years and kept upping the salary until I could no longer refuse," she said in her matter-of-fact manner. She gave in when the Hotel Sahara in Las Vegas indicated it would pay her $30,000 a week for a three-week appearance. Her timing was perfect. Las Vegas had grown up from the desert scrub as a wartime boom-town, offering rest and recreation to servicemen and high-rollers flush with money from the West Coast munitions industries: now, in peacetime, it needed stars like Dietrich to gain for itself an international reputation for style as well as high stakes. In a way, it was the perfect apotheosis of Lola-Lola, Frenchy, Erika von Schlütow, and all the other cabaret and salon "entertainers," high and low, that she had played on the screen: life now aped art and surpassed it.

She had always taken immense pains over her public appearance. In 1950, when merely asked to present an award at the "Oscar" ceremonies, her "intelligence unit" had informed her of the red, white and blue decor of the event. "In which case, Mama will wear black," she decreed. And Mama gained an ovation, slinking across the stage in a Dior dress that looked airbrushed on to her, but whose chaste full-length sleeves were impudently contradicted by a vertical slit that allowed a "now you see it, now you don't" flash of calf as she moved. Her main concern at the rehearsal was to learn from which side she would make her *entrée*: the Dior cutter would be given his instructions accordingly. For Las Vegas, it was the couturier Jean Louis who had to endure weeks of having his creations ripped apart and resewn until she was satisfied. The $8,000 gown she wore at the first performance at the Sahara, in December 1953, created a sensation. Made of black

In *Rancho Notorious,* directed by Fritz Lang (shown explaining a fine point in the action to his leading lady), Dietrich's "deadpan mask hid the boredom she was feeling." The insets picture Dietrich in conversation with director Alfred Hitchcock during the making of *Stage Fright* and sharing a scene from *No Highway in the Sky* with her *Destry* co-star James Stewart.

net and sequins, and worn with a full-length redingote trimmed with twelve feet of white fur, it gave the impression that she was virtually nude from the waist up. No bra could be seen. At the photo session before the show, flashbulb lighting intensified the illusion of nakedness. Dietrich protested (though not over much) that the effect on people would have been the same had she worn a black sweater. For the latter part of her act at the Sahara, she switched to an abbreviated ringmaster outfit with scarlet tailcoat and topper. The lighting remained Von Sternberg's; the effect was all Marlene's.

But what was sensational was not simply the vision, but the sound that came with it. A surprising sound for many in those early audiences. For Dietrich did not sing so much as act the lyrics of her songs. She practically spoke them in her mezzo-baritone, with a range of barely more than an octave and a half, giving an impression which dramatically colored the meaning of the words. Later she was to say that she picked her repertoire for the words, not the melodies. This style caused some confusion among the press people present. Not many of them were music critics. They were not acquainted with the technique of the European *Sprechtsinger*, or *diseuse* to use the more melodic French word, which consists of the entertainer speaking on tone and using words and emotions to connect subtly with the audience's deepest feelings. "She has no great voice," wrote Dick Williams, of the New York *Mirror*, who was present, adding, almost as compensation, "but she has an adroit beguiling style."[47] This judgment scarcely conceals a certain perplexity typical of other reviews; and there is evidence that Dietrich felt her act had been somewhat misunderstood, for she wrote a note to Hedda Hopper on December 17, 1953—retained in that columnist's archives in the Motion Picture Academy library—to thank her for what *she* had written and saying, "You understood what I attempted with this appearance—the others didn't, it seems. I send you love—Marlene." The "others" very quickly did their music homework; and Dietrich's style, in which the story carries the song the way she carries the whole show, by the precision of the words and the aural implication of their emotional resonances, was hailed as a marvelously effective and winning way of bringing a legend to the people—though not too close to the people.

With Dietrich as *diseuse*, one kept one's distance—gratefully. Her act was calculated to instill awe as well as adulation. She never risked placing herself at a disadvantage: one sharp-eyed newsman, covering the rare press conference that she could occasionally be persuaded to hold by a very persuasive impresario, noted that she never sat down. That might have been something to do with the inches that age gathers around even the best-exercised midriff: but it serves to remind us that she considered herself always "on parade," taking the salute as it were, manifesting the same degree of discipline as she expected of her troops but rarely received from the general slump of the press corps, whom she made no secret of detesting even when she agreed to meet with them. (Her special contempt was reserved for those reporters whose knowledge of her, she sensed,

The third transfiguration of Marlene Dietrich: nightclub and concert entertainer. The photograph by John Engstead shows her as she appeared at the Sahara, Las Vegas, in December 1953.

had been formed by library clippings rather than the influence of her own spell: it was the old soldier's contempt for the rookie war correspondent.)

Wherever she performed in the years following her Las Vegas debut, no matter what world capital, country or continent, Dietrich's act scarcely varied. True, she chose her "narration" to suit the language of her audience. Sometimes she would make language itself an emotional issue. Witness her determination to sing in German on her 1960 tour of Israel, in defiance of the official ban on that tongue. The interdiction offended her sense of logic: if *she* was not above suspicion, after a lifetime in which her Aryan German steadfastness had opposed the Nazis, and by logical extension supported the Jews, then who was? She sang in German and got an ovation.

What kept her act fresh was its unvarying discipline. Typically, Art Buchwald, reviewing her London appearance at the Café de Paris in 1954, singled out the inflexible protocol she imposed on everyone from waiters (no table service while she was on) to guests (no interval to break her spell). "How do you make such a quick change from the chiffon to the tailcoat?" Buchwald asked. Her reply showed the split-second underpinning of the illusion. "First . . . I throw off my shoes and then I throw off the gown. I take off my earrings and rings, dry my lips and grab two hairbrushes full of brilliantine and put down my hair. Then I put on socks, shirt, pants, suspenders and zip up my pants. The girl gives me my coat. I ring the buzzer for the orchestra, jump into my shoes, put on my hat, and I'm ready. The whole thing takes a minute."[48] Some of the men's clothes were, of course, "breakaway" stage garments—that is to say, tailored with an invisible slit down the back so that she could practically walk into them. But in the early days, she found one item frustratingly recalcitrant. "The socks," she told a Las Vegas reporter, "I haven't found any way to put on the socks differently. I still have to bend over and pull them on." Maybe by the time Buchwald spoke to her, she had brought the socks to heel.

If a chorus line supported her act, it was said that the girls had instructions to kick only so high. Dietrich, to the marvel of many, would then be seen kicking higher than these young girls. The illusion was what mattered.

The report persists that Dietrich's surprisingly resilient walk when she was in her fifties and sixties was aided by a form-fitting, flesh-colored undergarment made of latex rubber. Milo Anderson, designer of many stars' wardrobes from the 1930s to the mid-1950s, has recently reminded us of the importance that Dietrich attached to a good foundation. "We had one foundation garment in *Manpower* [which Warners made in 1941] that we fitted for a week, and she still wouldn't accept it. Finally, she said, 'You had better call Irene at Bullocks Wilshire. [Irene, successor to Adrian at MGM, later ran a salon at the Los Angeles department store.] So I called her up and explained the problem. She said, 'You're doing it just the way I would: stick to your guns, Milo.' Years later I was in some grubby nightclub in Paris when somebody touched my shoulder, and it was Marlene. She took me aside to show me the most marvelous foundation garment. It came up to her neck and went out to her arm and put everything in just the right place. It was so dark, I couldn't see how it was made. Suddenly she was gone. I never saw her again."[49]

For someone like the London *Sunday Times*'s theater critic, Harold Hobson, who was "never a devotee of Piaf's little black dress," the illusion was wonderfully sustained whatever underpinnings might have been revealed to her dresser (Dietrich jubilantly sent a clipping of his review to Hedda Hopper). It was so vital for her to play upon an audience that the *quality* of the audience was important to her, and anything that intervened between her and the audience was anathema to her. This is largely why she held off appearing on television until Alexander Cohen paid her $250,000 to sing fourteen songs for a TV special screened in America in 1973. "I don't like people watching me for free," she complained, showing that although money filled her purse, it did not shut her mouth. By "free" she did not mean TV viewers. She referred to the specially *invited* people making up the audience at the TV taping: they were not like those fervent devotees who stood in line for hours at the box office in the hope of a returned ticket; they were not a "young" audience; they were "stuffy." And television, with its overriding concern for speed, was an "unprofessional" medium: it had no time to do things "her way."

As she grew older, too, something else was introduced into her performances that fused her own uniqueness with the commonplaceness of Everyman. Jack Kroll put it perfectly when he wrote: "Dietrich's beauty blended with her mortality to make a poignant if at times disturbing event."[50] It is wrong to say she stayed ageless: it was the very sense of Dietrich—even she!—running out of time that enveloped her with a preciousness. This might be the last time one would see her . . . there would be no successor. In such a heightened sense of expectation—of trepidation, almost—did she perform; and invariably she triumphed.

Though "sex" was never directly employed in the illusion, she used to say that she did the first half of her show, clad in wispy or shimmering gowns, for men; the second half, when she did her quick-change into top hat and tails, was for the girls. Actually it was by no means schematized: the division only served to put a slightly impudent gloss on the ambiguous sexuality that the illusionist found useful to maintain. The strangely low register of her voice gave the effect of lullaby to many of her songs, even though the actual sentiments were frequently sensual ones: like the sexual innuendos of "Jonny," or the camp-follower attachments of "Lili Marlene," or the anticipation she created, with such delicious duplicity, by announcing that now she would sing "the song that made me famous"—whereupon someone was sure to call out "Falling in Love Again," only to be coyly chided, "No, no, no . . . not that one—the *other* one," and someone else, possibly planted in the audience, would yell "Lola" and launch Dietrich into the tantalizing naughtiness of that lyric. But she always took care to end on a note that began to sound more like a tribute to her admirers' stamina than a character reference for a *femme fatale*—"Falling in Love Again."

Dietrich's tours as a "live" performer took her from Las Vegas (*opposite*) to London's Café de Paris (*right*) and the Théâtre de l'Etoile in Paris (*below*). Crowds of admirers were on hand wherever she went (*inset, opposite*).

Above all, Dietrich's was the voice seemingly tailor made for every Armistice Day—her songs of war and despair filling the commemorative minute with universal remembrance. As Peter Bogdanovich wrote, after hearing her, "A folk song, 'Go 'Way From My Window,' has never been done with such passion, and in her hands 'Where Have All the Flowers Gone?' is not just another anti-war lament, but a tragic accusation against us all."[51] As Graham Greene put it, hearing her icily dispassionate account of her war service that took no sides but only listed the countries she passed through in the wake of battle, "She is the marble motive for heroisms and sacrifices."

Nor should one forget the orchestrations of Burt Bacharach, and his successors, which gave the stage act its melodic unity—or, as she put it herself, "its soul." Bacharach she called "my teacher, my critic, my accompanist, my conductor and my arranger." He was also the flame that burned in the ice.

Dietrich returned to films, among a cluster of first and second magnitude stars, in Mike Todd's *Around the World in 80 Days* (1956), enlivening David Niven's San Francisco stopover in the film as a dance-hall queen in a saloon bar where Frank Sinatra is the pianist. So little: but so good. But then she did what no one of her charm should ever have allowed herself to do. She fell victim to another charmer in the person of Vittorio de Sica, whose conman's skill as co-star of *The Monte Carlo Story* (1957) was not slick enough to deceive the eye into enjoying the tedious tale of two born gamblers who are out to fleece the wealthy and wind up winning each other. Her own boredom during the shooting of the casino scenes that took an age to arrange showed itself in a perverse preference for just the opposite kind of role. "Give me a role where I can grovel in the dust," she said, "then I'm happy. You have to work so much harder to convince the public that you're suffering when your gloves and handbag match."[52] Lubitsch would have applauded that: too bad he was beyond reach.

But just when it looked that Dietrich's film career had once again petered out, she appeared in *Witness for the Prosecution* (1958), a *de luxe* edition of Agatha Christie's mystery melodrama, playing the wife who risks her neck for her man—a death sentence hanging around in the vicinity always seemed to bring out the best in her. Save for one dubious moment of plot mechanics, she was featured throughout in chilly magnificence by director Billy Wilder. Her entry into the chambers of the eminent attorney, played by Charles Laughton, is wonderfully climaxed—her straight tweeds, stiffly waved hair, a voice sounding like a tuning fork struck on an icicle, a face as unwrinkled and expressionless as a frosted almond combine to make her appear less a woman than an apparition. Laughton gapes—*even Laughton*! And at once a plain case of murder sparkles with the allure of a *cause célèbre*.

Opinion, however, differs over the extent of Dietrich's success in transforming herself at the end of the film into a London skivvy with crooked teeth and a Cockney accent. It is hard to believe she could have fooled anyone unfamiliar with Christie's "surprise" denouement. Admittedly, this is a personal verdict, but

In the late 1950s, Dietrich's film career continued with *Witness for the Prosecution* (above), *Monte Carlo Story* (with Vittorio de Sica, *below, left*) and *Touch of Evil* (with co-star and director Orson Welles, *below, right*).

A tour of Germany in 1960 brought Dietrich in contact with her countrymen as an entertainer for the first time in thirty years. On stage at the Titania-Palast, Berlin, she acknowledges applause at the end of her show (*left*). Her return to Berlin was an occasion for renewing old ties and making new acquaintances. She crossed paths with her former mentor, Josef von Sternberg (*below*), encountered longtime fans in the street, signed the city's Golden Book for Mayor Willy Brandt and (*opposite, below*), posed for news photographers with a German actress of a younger generation, Hildegard Knef.

Goodbye to Berlin (*above*)
and hello to New York, 1960.

Wilder must have had his doubts, too, for he filmed the blackmailing phone call she makes twice over, once in makeup to retain the audience's surprise, and once without makeup with the probable aim of substituting suspense for surprise. He used the former—and the public agreed to be fooled.

As a cigarillo-smoking brothel madam, wearing a tentacular black wig, originally fashioned for an Elizabeth Taylor film, that she had found in a dressing-room closet, she appeared with Orson Welles that same year in the latter's *Touch of Evil* (1958), speaking the obituary line about the corrupt but carnally empathetic cop whom Welles also played: "He was some kind of man . . . but what does it matter *what* you say about people?" She liked quoting that line in later years. Out of context, it might be: but she found it apposite whenever she gave one of her increasingly rare interviews to the media.

Her last role of any distinction was in Stanley Kramer's *Judgment at Nuremberg* (1961), as the German general's widow who represents the unashamed face of militarism that refuses to be judged by the victors' tribunal. Why did Dietrich take such an ambiguous part? It was said that she hoped to bring home to Germans the dangerous hold that Nazism retained on their imaginations. But in the film it does not work out like that at all. The casting destroys the intention. The star's own lifelong endorsement of the warrior myth—though certainly not the "superman" myth—heavily and nostalgically overplays the role's judgmental purpose. Dietrich's very presence subverts the message. She endows German militarism with nobility—vicarious, admittedly—but nobility all the same.

The message was carried more directly to the heart and ears of the ex-enemy (and, one hopes, the mind: though even here there is a doubt) by her tour of Germany in 1960. It was the first time she had faced her countrymen as an entertainer singing in their language since 1930. Before the trip, she was unwontedly nervous. There had been talk of demonstrations against her—her words about the Germans having had it coming to them still rankled—and threats of eggs and tomatoes splattering against that cool facade. ("It's not the tomatoes I fear," she was reported as saying, "but the eggs: their stains never wash out." It apparently never entered her mind to anticipate bloodshed: or perhaps it did, but she may have comforted herself by thinking that at least bloodstains washed out!) The threat of confrontation never materialized—her Prussian presence outfaced the unruly handful at her concerts. "One was thankful," said a close friend, "she was on our side during the war, not Hitler's."

The Black Fox (1962), a documentary account of Hitler's career which she narrated, spelled out in prose, delivered dispassionately but with subtlety, all the feelings about Fascism which she had had to restrain while her family remained under its threat. She gave the film a tone that helped it win a 1962 "Oscar" (for the best feature-length documentary).

Dietrich's concert tours continued. She had done South America in 1959, where the masses received her like a Blue Angel of the Annunciation; and Paris fell to her the same year; from then on, it was like a one-woman army, though few

armies marched to victory on such deliciously sly rations of publicity. One trick she had was to be photographed arriving at a capital's airport carrying a very small, though expensive looking, package. The personage greeting her—perhaps a luminary of the same wattage as herself, Coward, Chevalier, Jean-Pierre Aumont, or whoever—offers to carry it. She declines. He persists. By now everyone (i.e., the press) is clamoring to know what is in the minuscule container she guards so jealously. Her jewels? "No." Her vitamin pills? A disdainful look. Then what, Marlene, *what?* Whereupon, she pretends to take pity, holds up the tiny packet, and declares as the cameras flash: "It's the dress I'll be wearing in the show."

"Of all the tours you've done," Hedda Hopper asked her in 1965, "which impressed you most?" No hesitation. "Israel—that was the greatest!" Hedda Hopper's notes show Dietrich confiding her thoughts on Israel and its people to this columnist and close friend. But they are fascinating in another way, too. By analogy with the Israelis, Dietrich reveals her own attitudes regarding the family and the purposes of family life: in talking of Israeli children, she offers the most direct clue yet to the often puzzling circumstances surrounding her own child's early upbringing—and her own.

"I went [to Israel] on my own—I didn't go there to make money," she told Hopper, and proceeded to talk of it as a trip undertaken for education and inspiration. In the Jewish people she met, she admired a very Teutonic virtue. "They all work at something. The children are all taken care of by one person and the mother and father can work the land. Children are brought up by people who do not have the worries of daily life . . . they are brought up by people whose business it is to bring up children . . . [and are] not influenced by the moods of the wife or husband who are harassed at night when they come from work."

Whether or not this actually accorded with the Israeli practice of child rearing, it won approval from a woman who put the work ethic at least on the same level as family life, if not slightly higher. Viewed thus, her own unorthodox "family life" in her Hollywood years, with an absentee husband and a child reared by many hands other than the working mother's, becomes an understandable and even desirable arrangement. Children should be treated with respect, she insisted: in Israel, they were like "the holy cows in India." Perhaps "love" is part of that "respect," though the reference to husband and wife returning home out of sorts after the day's work is not reassuring—it is odd to find "harassment" associated with home life. It is not at all the customary picture of the "happy family."

But then "happiness" is a quality seldom dwelt on in Dietrich's (admittedly rare) public pronouncements. One is not sure whether she attached the same value to pursuing it as most people do: perhaps she would regard it as a human weakness, rather than a natural goal. What impressed her about Israelis was their discipline. And in that country, surrounded by the threat of encroaching enemies, their discipline reminded her of the early American settlers, pioneering people too, ever on the watch for hostile Indians: "The women in the covered wagons

Dietrich's "last role of distinction" was in Stanley Kramer's *Judgment at Nuremberg.* In it she plays the widow of a German general who has been executed for war crimes. The stills show her in conversation with Spencer Tracy (as the principal judge, *above*) and listening to testimony at the trials.

had to handle the guns and fight." In Israel, she said with approval, "the women
. . . must have army training. They all have an aim in life—all are working for
something higher."

There is no indication that Dietrich's praise of these "virtues" means she would
also endorse them as part of our way of life in the West. But her reactions and
opinions accord so closely with what one knows of her personal preferences, and
what one can infer from the opportunities that have shaped her career and have
helped form the world's image of her, that this candid approbation of national
virtues seems a just, if not generous, description of parts of her own nature.

But Hedda Hopper did not run classes in civics or moral philosophy: she soon
got her guest on to less elevated themes. How about pictures? she asked. A weary,
"Oh, if something interesting comes along." Well, they have all these Italian
broads in films—why not you? "Nobody's looking." (Can't we see Dietrich's
shrug of unconcern?) Who's your agent? "I have no agent . . . I haven't had one in
years. Besides, pictures couldn't bring me any more money than I have now."
Yes, said the unstoppable Miss Hopper, entirely missing the point, but you could
have something to play back some day. "I couldn't be more satisfied with what
I'm doing . . . I can sing all the sad songs I want to." What about *beaux*? "Oh, my
God, no. I'm working. I have no time." Her interrogator laid it on the line. When
have you seen Noël Coward? Whatever thoughts this query prompted, they were
not of undying love, but of more practical matters.

I saw him in London. He'd had his face lifted. He always told me that stuff about how I
had to age gracefully. He had his teeth out and insisted I have mine out, too. I said, "But
these are *my* teeth—why should I have them out?" But I have mine out, he'd say, and I'm
happy. I'd say, "Noël, don't give me that crap. So you had to have your teeth out, I'm
sorry. But don't tell me you're happy." When Binkie Beaumont [the London impresario]
told me he'd had his face lifted, I lay down on the floor and screamed with laughter. The
only way I would have my face lifted is if Elizabeth [Arden?] would do it. She'd know just
how much to pull up. I wouldn't trust any doctor to pull me into shape.

Dietrich had as few worries about status as she had about appearance. Instead
of putting up at the Beverly Wilshire or the Beverly Hills Hotel, she was staying in
a comfortable but small and undistinguished place, the Rodeo, on Rodeo Drive.
Why there? "It's next to my dentist."

The 1970s were painful years for Dietrich. In declining health, she suffered
several broken bones when she regrettably lost her balance on unfamiliar concert
stages. Where American cabaret artists once flatteringly imitated her, they now
cruelly caricatured her and the song that was her "signature." "Falling in Love
Again" became, on the satirist's lips, "Falling off Stage Again." Her friends
found her difficult to reach; when they did succeed, they suspected her of resisting
an intrusion into her private life by announcing (as if she were the maid, or other
aide, who had answered the telephone) that "Miss Dietrich has had to go to
Switzerland," or wherever. Old loyalties were severely strained by this
idiosyncratic behavior. Old friends began to die off. And some who were closer
than friends: her husband, Rudi Sieber, in 1976.

Two recording sessions:
narrating the soundtrack for
the film documentary *Black
Fox* (*above*) and taping an
album of her hit songs for
Columbia Records (*right*).

To the surprise of everyone who had thought her screen career was over, she made a brief appearance in *Just a Gigolo* (1978), a West German evocation of the economic and moral chaos of the Weimar Republic in which her art had first flowered: she played a baroness, heavily veiled, who commanded—the military metaphor still applied—a veritable army of handsome gigolos. She sang a short verse of the title song—and listened for the applause from the clientele at the Eden Hotel.

Her views on death were predictably stoic, dismissive even. Rex Reed asked her if it frightened her. "No, because all of my friends are dead already," she replied. "I guess you were sad when Judy Garland died," Reed persisted. "Oh, no, I was very happy. There was someone who wanted to die. If you want to die, go die. But don't be a bore about it."[53]

Mortality brought out the ironist in her when it was her own that came under discussion. She had long perfected what began as a private joke about her funeral and this was now turned into a veritable *chanson de geste* in its rollcall of the famous names whom she hoped would be present. Rudi Sieber had been cast as the funeral director who would supervise the service—at Notre Dame Cathedral. Representing the Queen of England would be Douglas Fairbanks, Jr.; Jean Gabin would be leaning against the cathedral door, cigarette dangling Gallically at the corner of his mouth; Hemingway would be carrying the ears of a freshly slain bull to lay on the catafalque; Erich Maria Remarque would have gone in error to the wrong funeral. Many another woman has let her mind roam over the men in her life. Trust Dietrich to enumerate the men at her death! She is reported, incidentally, to have planned a curtained-off section in the cathedral to corral her female acquaintances. Needless to say, deaths among this fantasized congregation meant that the joke began to pall, too.

Dietrich's last years have not been lived so much as lived out. In spite of being only a few years older than Garbo, she seems a star incredibly more aged and even more remote. Garbo in the early 1980s still "gets around," assisted by rich friends who extend to her the facilities that protect their own person and privacy whenever they travel. And Garbo is quite capable of traveling under her own steam, stumping down Second Avenue, bowed by arthritis but annealed against the curiosity of passers-by by time as well as age—and disguised by both, too. With Dietrich, things are cruelly different. From the very first day of international fame, she was a manufactured article. Oh, the components were unique. The way they were assembled was marvelous. The durability has been impressive. But Dietrich has always depended heavily, totally, upon the presentation of herself as Legend from a very early stage in her career. She did indeed become, in that much debased phrase, a *living* legend who had to look, move, talk, act and sing in a manner appropriate to her mythical nature. Most stars don't have to handle their legend, since it usually accretes around their memory and not their presence.

What has maintained Dietrich's legend so long is her innate discipline: that childhood training has lasted her well into old age even when her bones have

London, 1963: "The World's Most Glamorous Grandmother."

A brief appearance as a heavily veiled Prussian baroness in *Just a Gigolo* seems in all likelihood to have been Dietrich's swan song on the screen. The film's release in 1978 came exactly fifty-five years after her first German silent.

begun to let her down. Ernest Hemingway said of her that "the Kraut's the best that ever came into the ring." Staying power is as much a part of champions as winning; and Dietrich has had that. She has treated an exceptional career with exceptional coolness: there never seems to have been a moment of uninhibited surrender to the glamour she projected, no instance at all when the simple woman in her peeped out and winked at the legend. A certain humorlessness is, on the contrary, a part of her image. True, she debunked the image effectively in *Destry Rides Again* and in the sorority spawned by *Destry* of hardbitten hookers leading the male pack of brawny admirers in other films. But the effect depends more on loss of dignity than any sentimental surrender to human traits. MGM was able to mount a whole publicity campaign on a simple contradiction in terms epitomized by two words, "GARBO LAUGHS." One would be even more surprised to see a film advertised with the slogan "DIETRICH CHUCKLES." Her coolness has actually proved a good preservative. At a low temperature things last well, and she is no exception. Because contemporary film heroines—if any there are who answer to that description—generally involve themselves in life's events, a star like Dietrich who can afford the period luxury of standing well back and coolly surveying the world with uninvolved assurance is protected from our own changing standards. She dispensed with physical sexuality: her preference, and that of her mentor Von Sternberg, was for fateful attraction between the sexes. Even in the man's arms, she never seemed to have surrendered the prerogatives of her gender. Yes, certainly, some of her poses, her attitudes, her dialogue are greeted with gratified and audible pleasure by audiences today—not quite a send-up, but sometimes not far from it, either. Yet she herself escapes the verdict of mockery formed by camp fashion. She possesses perfect judgment of what makes eroticism entertaining and keeps it extraordinarily exclusive to herself. One may mock the period flavor: one does not mock Dietrich. Her voice has been one of the great instruments of controling audience reactions. Like Garbo's deep-souled tones, hers add an erotic dimension to her visual mystery. It is direct in a strangely masculine way, yet it goes with an emphatically glamorous woman. When the woman switches clothes and puts on male attire, the voice does not need to switch genders to complement the transvestite effect with ambiguous resonance.

One does not really think of Dietrich as an actress first and foremost—though that could be said of a lot of other stars, too, since stardom is achieved when a personality has been sufficiently rotated in a diverse number of roles to the point where one particular facet evokes an overwhelming public curiosity and enjoyment of its repeated and standardized display. Dietrich's fateful association with Von Sternberg insured that what he saw in her—and only that—would be what other people would see too. The films they made together were the ones that have lastingly defined her public image—though the gossipy nature of their creative collusion also counted for much of the initial fascination. Dietrich was an *imposed* star: she was not tried out in a variety of roles to see which clicked with the public. The erotic image manufactured out of her obedience to another man's fantasy was sufficiently strong to register the minute her international public glimpsed her in *The Blue Angel* and *Morocco*. Undoubtedly, the spell wore off: but by then the legend was potent enough to sustain her independent career; and when she finally took sole control of it by using the world as her concert platform, then she became an absolute ruler who had only herself to please.

Dietrich has never asked for sympathy, never wanted to be liked, never wished for love in the sense of the mutual commitment that a unique star and her worldwide audience make to each other. Pickford, Davis, Crawford and Swanson were all "loved" stars in this sense; Monroe was a loved and pitied star; even Garbo was loved and revered. But Dietrich never condescended to this vulgar pact. She owed her fans absolutely nothing. Nothing, except a good show. That was her "love." On what, then, does her stardom rest? First of all, on the way her obedient presence enabled her so-called discoverer to formulate a female species (ambiguous, sometimes, but that did no harm) who had no competitor in veiled mystery and predictable mood. What about Garbo?, one asks. The truth is, Garbo was always unpredictable: she had no need to wear a veil. Thought was Garbo's veil. Secondly, Dietrich's first international role allowed her to incarnate a character who is best remembered for that insidiously self-enraptured song, "Falling in Love Again." The haunting melody and lyrics allowed her to retain the strength of her siren personality right down to the present day. It recalled a kind of willful decadence associated with a relatively brief but still dangerously alluring period of German history. Dietrich is virtually our last link with the old High German style of life and with the type of mass entertainment enjoyed by pre-Hitlerite society. No wonder one of the West Berlin newspapers greeted her first postwar concert appearance in Germany's deposed capital city with the declaration that this was more than "a reunion with a woman who has about her the aura of Berlin . . . a reunion with a sound that was more than the effect of her singing. It was the sound of an epoch."

Lastly, her stardom has connotations of a *class*, the Prussian Junker class that, for all her carefully articulated "statelessness," Dietrich belongs to by sympathy if not precisely by birth. It is a class rooted in a code of conduct and a set of beliefs, and both conduct and beliefs were essentially based in military loyalties and lineage. For all that the songs she is partial to singing, or speaking, are the ones that decry war or console the warriors, Dietrich's commanding bearing projects the sympathies and expectations of a woman who is mother, lover and honorary colonel to the ranks of fighting men. One has traced these qualities throughout the films that defined her screen *persona* and seen them, literally, in action when she seized the opportunity provided by World War II to follow her men—much as, in the movies, she had followed her man. Reading her *jeu d'esprit* on the celebrated mourners she may have hoped to entice to her burial service, one wonders what the event will actually be like and reflects on how appropriate a military funeral would be for the lady.

For despite the flesh-colored Jean Louis gowns designed to provide such a startling *trompe l'oeil* of nudity, despite the white tie and tails she zips into to underline a cheeky gender switch, Dietrich wears her enduring stardom like a uniform cut to the military specifications of duty, discipline, loyalty to the regiment, and judicious detachment from all the rest of us rowdy civilians. "Now here's a song that is very close to my heart," she was wont to announce in those husky tones that sounded as if the dust of her wartime travels was still in her throat. "I sang it during the war. I sang it for three long years: all through Africa, Sicily, Italy; through Alaska, Greenland, Iceland; through England, through France, through Belgium and Holland, through Germany and into Czechoslovakia." The song is, of course, "Lili Marlene." The marching song of a very long life. When she departs it, one hopes that somewhere there will be a flag lowered to half-mast: it will be more becoming to her than any fade-out on the screen, any curtain on the stage.

ACKNOWLEDGMENTS

In addition to the names and sources noted in the text and the bibliography, my indebtedness for material on which to base this study of Marlene Dietrich encompasses individuals and institutions in various countries. In particular, I wish to thank Herr Dr Fritz Falk, director of the Schmuckmuseum at Pforzheim, West Germany, Frau Dr Barbara Mundt, research associate at the Kunstgewerbemuseum, Berlin, and Mr David Beasley, assistant to the librarian at the Worshipful Company of Goldsmiths, London, all of whom contributed to my knowledge of the jewelry business founded by the family of Dietrich's mother; Ms Carla Wartenberg, who helped me translate contemporary reviews and articles on Dietrich's German films; the curator and staff of the Margaret Herrick Library at the Academy of Motion Picture Arts and Sciences, Beverly Hills, California, and in particular Ms Carol Epstein, who helped me compress weeks of research into days by her astute sifting of documentary evidence, and Mr Sam Gill, who made available to me some of the publicly deposited papers from the library's Hedda Hopper Collection; the head librarian and staff at the British Film Institute Reference Library, London; the curator and staff of the National Film Archive, London, and in particular Ms Elaine Burrows, viewings supervisor, and Ms Liz Heasman, viewing service, who enabled me to see some of the rarer Dietrich films.

Not for the first time, Metro-Goldwyn-Mayer opened its enviably well-ordered archives to me. For the information I drew from them regarding Dietrich's brief but enlightening relationship with MGM, I am indebted to the assistance of Ms Karla Davidson, vice-president, general counsel, entertainment, Mr Herbert S. Nusbaum, attorney, Mrs Florence E. Warner, office manager, legal department, and Mr Ben Presser, head of legal files, all of MGM Film Co., Culver City, California. Ms Beatrix Miller, editor-in-chief, *Vogue* magazine, London, and her library staff, helped me trace Leo Lerman's penetrating wartime interview with Dietrich which appeared in the pages of American *Vogue*. Readers familiar with some of the best-written studies of cinema will appreciate the advice I was given by Mr Kevin Brownlow and Mr Richard Schickel, critics, historians and film-makers; and I am indebted to Mr Sam Jaffe, a Paramount executive when Dietrich was that studio's contract artist, for sharing his memories with me. Others who were (or are) close to Dietrich also recalled helpful characteristics of her as an artist and friend, and it is evidence of this star's unwaning influence that all of them declined the courtesy of being named here. Mr John Kobal provided most of the book's illustrations from his justly celebrated collection and I thank him and his associate, Mr Simon Crocker.

ALEXANDER WALKER

Taormina 1983—London 1984

FILMOGRAPHY

DER KLEINE NAPOLEON
(The Little Napoleon)
(Union-Film, 1923)

Napoleon Bonaparte: Egon von Hagen; *Jerome Bonaparte*: Paul Heidemann; *Georg von Melsungen*: Harry Liedtke; *Jeremias von Katzenellenbogen*: Jacob Tiedtke; *Charlotte*: Antonia Dietrich; *Liselotte*: Loni Nest; *Annemarie*: Alice Hechy; *Florian Wunderlich*: Kurt Vespermann; *Marshal*: Paul Biensfeld; *Director of the Royal Ballet*: Kurt Fuss; *Prima Ballerina*: Marquisette Bosky; *Kathrin*: Marlene Dietrich; *Valet*: Wilhelm Bendow.

Director: Georg Jacoby; *Script*: Robert Liebmann, Georg Jacoby.

TRAGÖDIE DER LIEBE
(Tragedy of Love)
(Joe May-Film, 1923)

Ombrade: Emil Jannings; *Musette*: Erika Glassner; *Countess Manon de Moreau*: Mia May; *The Judge*: Kurt Vespermann; *Lucie*: Marlene Dietrich.

Director: Joe May; *Script*: Lee Birinski, Adolf Lantz; *Cameramen*: Sophus Wangoe, Karl Puth; *Sets*: Paul Leni; *Costumes*: Ali Hubert; *Production Assistant*: Rudolf Sieber.

DER MENSCH AM WEGE
(The Man at the Roadside)
(Osmania-Film, 1923)

Schuster: Alexander Granach; *The Human Angel*: Wilhelm Dieterle; *with* Heinrich George, Wilhelm Völker, Emilie Unda, Marlene Dietrich, etc.

Director and script: Wilhelm Dieterle; *Cameraman*: Willy Hameister; *Assistant Cameraman*: Willi Habentz; *Sets*: Herbert Richter-Luckian.

DER SPRUNG INS LEBEN
(Leap into Life)
(Oskar Messter-Film, 1924)

A circus acrobat: Xeni Desni; *Her partner*: Walter Rilla; *A student*: Paul Heidemann; *His aunt*: Frida Richard; *The student's friend*: Kathe Haack; *The Ringmaster*: Leonhard Haskel; *with* Olga Engl, Marlene Dietrich, and Hans Brausewetter.

Director: Johannes Guter; *Producer*: Oskar Messter; *Script*: Franz Schulz; *Photographer*: Fritz Arno Wagner; *Sets*: Rudi Feldt.

DIE FREUDLOSE GASSE
(Joyless Street)
(Hirschal-Sofar-Film, 1925)

Josef Rumfort: Jaro Furth; *Grete Rumfort*: Greta Garbo; *Mariandl*: Loni Nest; *Maria Lechner*: Asta Nielsen; *with* Max Kohlhase, Silvia Torf *and* Marlene Dietrich (*who was unbilled*).

Director: G. W. Pabst; *Script*: Willi Haas; *Cameramen*: Guido Seeber, Curt Oertel and Walter Robert Lach; *Sets*: Hans Sohnle, Otto Erdmann; *Assistant Director*: Marc Sorkin; *Editor*: Anatol Litvak.

MANON LESCAUT
(UFA, 1926)

Manon Lescaut: Lya de Putti; *Des Grieux*: Vladimir Gaidarov; *Maréchal des Grieux*: Eduard Rothauser; *Marquis de Bli*: Fritz Greiner; *De Bli's son*: Hubert von Meyerinck; *Manon's aunts*: Frida Richard, Emilie Kurtz; *Susanne*: Lydia Potechina; *Tiberge*: Theodor Loos; *Lescaut*: Siegfried Arno; *Claire*: Trude Hesterberg; *Micheline*: Marlene Dietrich.

Director: Arthur Robison; *Script*: Hans Kyser, Arthur Robison; *Cameraman*: Theodor Sparkuhl; *Sets and costumes*: Paul Leni.

EINE DU BARRY VON HEUTE
(A Modern Du Barry)
(Felsom-Film, 1926)

Toinette: Maria Corda; *Sillon*: Alfred Abel; *Cornelius Corbett*: Friedrich Kayssler; *General Padilla*: Julius von Szöreghy; *Sandro, King of Asturia*: Jean Bradin; *Darius Kerbelian*: Hans Albers; *Count Rabbatz*: Alfred Gerasch; *Clairet*: Alfred Paulig; *Theater Director*: Hans Wassmann; *A servant*: Karl Platen; *Levasseur*: Eugen Burg; *A coquette*: Marlaine *(sic)* Dietrich.

Director: Alexander Korda; *Script*: Robert Liebmann, Alexander Korda, Paul Reboux; *Cameraman*: Fritz Arno Wagner; *Sets*: Otto Friedrich Werndorff.

MADAME WÜNSCHT KEINE KINDER
(Madame Doesn't Want Children)
(Fox Europa-Film, 1926)

Elyane Parizot: Maria Corda; *Paul le Barroy*: Harry Liedtke; *Louise Bonvin*: Maria Paudler; *Elyane's mother*: Trude Hesterberg.

Director: Alexander Korda; *Script*: Adolf Lantz, Bela Balazs; *Cameramen*: Theodor Sparkuhl, Robert Baberske; *Sets*: Otto Friedrich Werndorff; *Producer*: Karl Freund; *Associate Producer*: Karl Hartl; *Production Assistant*: Rudolf Sieber.

HOPF HOCH, CHARLY!
(Head Up, Charly!)
(Ellen Richter-Film, 1926)

Frank Ditmar: Anton Pointner; *'Charly' Ditmar*: Ellen Richter; *John Jacob Bunjes*: Michael Bohnen; *Harry Moshenheim*: Max Gulsdorff; *Margie Quinn*: Margerie Quimby; *Rufus Quinn*: George de Carlton; *Marquis d'Ormesson*: Angelo Ferrari; *Duke of Sanzedilla*: Robert Scholz; *Prince Platonoff*: Nikolai Malikoff; *Frau Zangenberg*: Toni Tetzlaff; *Edmée Marchand*: Marlene Dietrich; *The seamstress*: Blandine Ebinger.

Director: Willi Wolff; *Script*: Robert Liebmann, Willi Wolff; *Cameraman*: Axel Graatkjar; *Sets*: Ernst Stern.

DER JUXBARON (The Bogus Baron)
(Ellen Richter-Film, 1927)

The "Baron": Reinhold Schünzel; *Hugo Windisch*: Henry Bender; *Zerline Windisch*: Julia Serda; *Sophie*: Marlene Dietrich; *Hans von Grabow*: Teddy Bill; *Hilda von Grabow*: Colette Brettl; *Baron von Kimmel*: Albert Paulig; *Fränze*: Trude Hesterberg.

Director: Willi Wolff; *Scripts*: Robert Liebmann, Willi Wolff; *Cameraman*: Axel Graatkjar; *Sets*: Ernst Stern.

SEIN GRÖSSTER BLUFF
(His Greatest Bluff)
(Nero-Film, 1927)

Henry/Harry Devall: Harry Piel; *Madame Andersson*: Tony Tetzlaff; *Tilly*: Lotte Lorring; *Mimikry*: Albert Pauling; *Hennessy*: Fritz Greiner; *"Count" Koks*: Charly Berger; *Sherry*: Boris Michailow; *Yvette*: Marlene Dietrich.

Director: Harry Piel; *Script*: Henrik Galeen; *Cameramen*: Georg Muschner, Gotthardt Wolf; *Sets*: W. A. Herrmann.

CAFÉ ELECTRIC
(Sascha-Film, Austria, 1927)

Göttlinger: Fritz Alberti; *Erni*: Marlene Dietrich; *A friend of Erni*: Anny Coty; *Ferdl*: Willi Forst.

Director: Gustav Ucicky; *Script*: Jacques Bachrach; *Cameraman*: Hans Androschin; *Sets*: Artur Berger.

PRINZESSIN OLALA (Princess Olala)
(Super-Film, 1928)

The Prince: Hermann Böttcher; *Prince Boris*: Walter Rilla; *The Chamberlain*: Georg Alexander; *Princess Xenia*: Carmen Boni; *Hedy*: Ila Meery; *Chicotte de Gastoné*: Marlene Dietrich; *René*: Hans Albers.

Director: Robert Land; *Script*: Franz Schulz, Robert Land; *Cameraman*: Willi Goldberger; *Sets*: Robert Neppach.

ICH KÜSSE IHRE HAND, MADAME
(I Kiss Your Hand, Madame)
(Super-Film, 1929)

Jacques: Harry Liedtke; *Laurence Gerard*: Marlene Dietrich; *Adolf Gerard*: Pierre de Guingand; *Tallandier*: Karl Huszar-Puffy.

Director: Robert Land; *Assistant Director*: Friedel Buckow; *Script*: Robert Land; *Cameramen*: Karl Drews, Gotthardt Wolf; *Assistant Cameramen*: Fritz Brunn, Fred Zinnemann; *Sets*: Robert Neppach. *Title song by* Ralph Erwin *(Music)* and Fritz Rotter *(Lyrics)*.

DIE FRAU, NACH DER MAN SICH SEHNT
(The Woman One Longs For)
(Terra-Film, 1929)

Stascha: Marlene Dietrich; *Dr Karoff*: Fritz Kortner; *Mrs Leblanc*: Frida Richard; *Charles Leblanc*: Oskar Sima; *Henry Leblanc*: Uno Henning.

Director: Kurt Bernhardt; *Script*: Ladislas Vajda; *Cameraman*: Kurt Courant; *Sets*: Robert Neppach.

DAS SCHIFF DER VERLORENEN MENSCHEN
(Ship of Lost Souls)
(Max Glass-Wengeroff-Film Production, 1929)

Captain Fernando Vela: Fritz Kortner; *Miss Ethel*: Marlene Dietrich; *Morian*: Gaston Modot; *T. W. Cheyne*: Robin Irvine.

Director: Maurice Tourneur; *Producer*: Max Glass; *Script*: Maurice Tourneur; *Cameraman*: Nikolaus Farkas; *Sets*: Franz Schroedter; *Assistant Director*: Jacques Tourneur.

GEFAHREN DER BRAUTZEIT
(Dangers of the Engagement Period)
(Strauss-Film, 1929)

Baron van Geldern: Willi Forst; *Evelyne*: Marlene Dietrich; *Yvette*: Lotte Lorring; *Florence*: Elza Temary; *McClure*: Ernst Stahl-Nachbaur; *Miller*: Bruno Ziener.

Director: Fred Sauer; *Script*: Walter Wassermann, Walter Schlee; *Cameraman*: László Schaffer; *Sets*: Max Heilbronner.

DER BLAUE ENGEL
(The Blue Angel)
(Erich Pommer Production; UFA, 1930)

Professor Immanuel Rath: Emil Jannings; *Lola-Lola/Fröhlich*: Marlene Dietrich; *Kiepert*: Kurt Gerron; *Guste*: Rosa Valetti; *Mazeppa*: Hans Albers; *The clown*: Reinhold Bernt; *Director of the school*: Eduard von Winterstein; *Beadle*: Hans Roth; *Students*: Rolf Muller (*Angst*), Rolant Varno (*Lohmann*), Karl Balhaus (*Ertzum*) and Robert Klein-Lork (*Goldstaub*); *The publican*: Karl Huszar-Puffy; *The captain*: Wilhelm Diegelmann; *The policeman*: Gerhard Bienert; *Rath's housekeeper*: Ilse Fürstenberg.

Director: Josef von Sternberg; *Producer*: Erich Pommer; *Script*: Robert Liebmann; *Cameramen*: Gunther Rittau, Hans Schneeberger; *Sets*: Otto Hunte, Emil

Hasler; *Editor*: Sam Winston; *Music*: Friedrich Holländer; *Sound*: Fritz Thiery; *Orchestra*: Weintraub's Syncopators; *Songs*: Friedrich Holländer *and* Robert Liebmann, *English lyrics by* Sam Lerner.

MOROCCO
(Paramount, 1930)

Tom Brown: Gary Cooper; *Amy Jolly*: Marlene Dietrich; *Kennington*: Adolphe Menjou; *Adjutant Caesar*: Ullrich Haupt; *Anna Dolores*: Juliette Compton; *Corporal Tatoche*: Francis McDonald; *Colonel Quinnevieres*: Albert Conti; *Madame Caesar*: Eve Southern; *Barratire*: Michael Visarof; *Lo Tinto*: Paul Porcaasi; *with* Emile Chautard.

Director: Josef von Sternberg; *Script*: Jules Furthman; *Photographer*: Lee Garmes; *Art Director*: Hans Dreier; *Costumes*: Travis Banton; *Editor*: Sam Winston; *Songs*: "Give Me the Man" *by* Leo Robin *and* Karl Hajos; "Quand l'Amour Meurt" *by* Cremieux.

DISHONORED
(Paramount, 1931)

X-27: Marlene Dietrich; *Lieutenant Kranau*: Victor McLaglen; *Colonel Kevrin*: Lew Cody; *Head of Secret Service*: Gustav von Seyffertitz; *General von Hindau*: Warner Oland.

Director: Josef von Sternberg; *Script*: D. H. Rubin; *Photographer*: Lee Garmes; *Music*: Karl Hajos; *Costumes*: Travis Banton; *Sound*: Harry D. Mills.

SHANGHAI EXPRESS
(Paramount, 1932)

Shanghai Lily: Marlene Dietrich; *Captain Donald Harvey*: Clive Brook; *Hui Fei*: Anna May Wong; *Henry Chang*: Warner Oland; *Sam Salt*: Eugene Pallette; *Mr Carmichael*: Lawrence Grant; *Mrs Haggerty*: Louise Closser Hale; *Eric Baum*: Gustav von Seyffertitz; *Major Lenard*: Emile Chautard.

Director: Josef von Sternberg; *Script*: Jules Furthman; *Photographer*: Lee Garmes; *Art Director*: Hans Dreier; *Music*: W. Franke Harling; *Costumes*: Travis Banton.

BLONDE VENUS
(Paramount, 1932)

Helen Faraday: Marlene Dietrich; *Edward Faraday*: Herbert Marshall; *Nick Townsend*: Cary Grant; *Johnny Faraday*: Dickie Moore.

Director: Josef von Sternberg; *Script*: Jules Furthman and S. K. Lauren; *Photographer*:

Bert Glennon; *Art Director*: Wiard Ihnen; *Music*: Oscar Potoker; *Costumes*: Travis Banton.

THE SONG OF SONGS
(Paramount, 1933)

Lily Czepanek: Marlene Dietrich; *Waldow*: Brian Aherne; *Baron von Merzbach*: Lionel Atwill; *Frau Rasmussen*: Alison Skipworth.

Director and Producer: Rouben Mamoulian; *Script*: Leo Birinski, Samuel Hoffenstein; *Photographer*: Victor Milner; *Costumes*: Travis Banton; *Music*: Karl Hajos, Milan Roder; *Song*: "Jonny" *by* Frederick Hollander, *English lyrics by* Edward Heyman.

THE SCARLET EMPRESS
(Paramount, 1934)

Catherine the Great: Marlene Dietrich; *Count Alexei*: John Lodge; *Grand Duke Peter*: Sam Jaffe; *Empress Elizabeth*: Louise Dresser; *Catherine as a child*: Maria Sieber; *Prince August*: C. Aubrey Smith.

Director: Josef von Sternberg; *Script*: Manuel Komroff; *Photographer*: Bert Glennon; *Art Directors*: Hans Dreier, Peter Ballbusch, Richard Kollorsz; *Costumes*: Travis Banton; *Special Effects*: Gordon Jennings.

THE DEVIL IS A WOMAN
(Paramount, 1935)

Concha Perez: Marlene Dietrich; *Don Pasqual*: Lionel Atwill; *Antonio Galvan*: Cesar Romero; *Don Paquito*: Edward Everett Horton; *Signora Perez*: Alison Skipworth.

Director and Photographer: Josef von Sternberg; *Script*: John Dos Passos, S. K. Winston; *Assistant Photographer*: Lucien Ballard; *Art Director*: Hans Dreier; *Costumes*: Travis Banton; *Editor*: Sam Winston; *Songs*: "(If It Isn't Pain) Then It Isn't Love" *and* "Three Sweethearts Have I" *by* Lee Robin *and* Ralph Rainger.

DESIRE
(Paramount, 1936)

Madeleine de Beaupré: Marlene Dietrich; *Tom Bradley*: Gary Cooper; *Carlos Margoli*: John Halliday; *Mr Gibson*: William Frawley; *Aristide Duval*: Ernest Cossart; *Dr Edouard Pauquet*: Alan Mowbray; *Police officer*: Akim Tamiroff.

Director: Frank Borzage; *Producer*: Ernst Lubitsch; *Script*: Edwin Justus Mayer, Waldemar Young, Samuel Hoffenstein;

Photographer: Charles Lang; *Art Directors*: Travis Banton; *Song*: "Awake in a Dream" *by* Frederick Hollander *and* Leo Rubin.

THE GARDEN OF ALLAH
(Selznick-International, released through United Artists, 1936)

Domini Enfilden: Marlene Dietrich; *Boris Androvsky*: Charles Boyer; *Count Anteoni*: Basil Rathbone; *Father Roubier*: C. Aubrey Smith; *Irena*: Tilly Losch; *Batouch*: Joseph Schildkraut; *Sand diviner*: John Carradine; *De Trevignac*: Alan Marshall.

Director: Richard Boleslawski; *Producer*: David O. Selznick; *Script*: W. P. Lipscomb, Lynn Riggs; *Photographer*: W. Howard Greene; *Photographic Advisor*: Harold Rosson; *Music*: Max Steiner; *Production designer*: Lansing C. Holden; *Art Directors*: Sturges Carne, Lyle Wheeler, Edward Boyle; *Costumes*: Ernst Dryden; *Editors*: Hal C. Kern, Anson Stevenson; *Sound*: Earl A. Wolcott; *Special Effects*: Jack Cosgrove; *Color Supervisor*: Natalie Kalmus.

KNIGHT WITHOUT ARMOR
(Alexander Korda-London Films, released through United Artists, 1937)

Alexandra: Marlene Dietrich; *A. J. Fotheringill*: Robert Donat; *Duchess*: Irene Vanburgh; *Vladinoff*: Herbert Lomas; *Colonel Adraxine*: Austin Trevor; *Axelstein*: Basil Gill; *Maronin*: David Tree; *Poushkoff*: John Clements.

Director: Jacques Feyder; *Producer*: Alexander Korda; *Script*: Lajos Biro, Arthur Wimperis; *Adaptation*: Frances Marion; *Photographer*: Harry Stradling; *Camera Operator*: Jack Cardiff; *Sets*: Lazare Meerson; *Costumes*: George Benda; *Music*: Miklos Rosza; *Music Director*: Muir Matheson; *Special Effects*: Ned Mann; *Editor*: Francis Lyon; *Recording Director*: A. W. Watkins; *Technical Adviser*: Roman Goul.

ANGEL
(Paramount, 1937)

Maria Barker: Marlene Dietrich; *Sir Frederick Barker*: Herbert Marshall; *Anthony Halton*: Melvyn Douglas; *Graham*: Edward Everett Horton; *Walton*: Ernest Cossart; *Grand Duchess Anna Dmitrievna*: Laura Hope Crews.

Director: Ernst Lubitsch; *Script*: Samson Raphaelson; *Photographer*: Charles Lang; *Costumes*: Travis Banton; *Special Effects*: Farciot Edouart; *Music*: Frederick Hollander; *Art Directors*: Hans Dreier, Robert Usher; *Editor*: William Shea; *Sound*: Harry Mills, Louis Messnkop; *Song*: "Angel" *by* Frederick Hollander *and* Leo Robin.

DESTRY RIDES AGAIN
(Universal, 1939)

Frenchy: Marlene Dietrich; *Tom Destry*: James Stewart; *Wash Dimsdale*: Charles Winninger; *Boris Callahan*: Mischa Auer; *Kent*: Brian Donlevy; *Lilybelle Callahan*: Una Merkel.

Director: George Marshall; *Producer*: Joe Pasternak; *Script*: Felix Jackson, Henry Meyers, Gertrude Purcell; *Photographer*: Hal Mohr; *Marlene Dietrich's Costumes*: Vera West; *Art Director*: Jack Otterson; *Musical Director*: Charles Previn; *Music*: Frank Skinner; *Editor*: Milton Carruth; *Sound*: Bernard B. Brown; *Assistant Director*: Vernon Keays; *Songs*: "Little Joe the Wrangler"; "You've Got That Look (That Leaves Me Weak)"; "The Boys in the Back Room" *by* Frederick Hollander *and* Frank Loesser.

SEVEN SINNERS
(Universal, 1940)

Bijou: Marlene Dietrich; *Bruce*: John Wayne; *Little Ned*: Broderick Crawford; *Sasha*: Mischa Auer; *Dr Martin*: Albert Dekker; *Tony*: Billy Gilbert; *Antro*: Oscar Homolka; *Dorothy*: Anna Lee.

Director: Tay Garnett; *Producer*: Joe Pasternak; *Script*: John Meehan, Harry Tugend; *Photographer*: Rudolph Mate; *Art Director*: Jack Otterson; *Marlene Dietrich's costumes*: Irene; *Costumes*: Vera West; *Music*: Frank Skinner; *Musical Director*: Charles Previn; *Sound*: Bernard B. Brown; *Songs*: "I've Been In Love Before"; "I Fall Overboard"; "The Man's In the Navy" *by* Frederick Hollander *and* Frank Loesser.

THE FLAME OF NEW ORLEANS
(Universal, 1941)

Claire Ledux: Marlene Dietrich; *Robert Latour*: Bruce Cabot; *Charles Giraud*: Roland Young; *Zolotov*: Mischa Auer; *First Sailor*: Andy Devine; *Second Sailor*: Frank Jenks; *Third Sailor*: Eddie Quillan; *Auntie*: Laura Hope Crews; *Bellows*: Franklin Pangborn.

Director: René Clair; *Producer*: Joe Pasternak; *Script*: Norman Krasna; *Photographer*: Rudolph Mate; *Music*: Frank Skinner; *Musical Director*: Charles Previn; *Art Directors*: Jack Otterson, Martin Obzina, Russell

A. Gausman; *Costumes*: René Hubert; *Editor*: Frank Gross; *Sound*: Bernard B. Brown; *Songs*: "Sweet as the Blush of May"; "Salt o'the Sea"; "Oh, Joyous Day" *by* Charles Previn *and* Sam Lerner.

MANPOWER
(Warner Bros.-First National, 1941)

Hank McHenry: Edward G. Robinson; *Fay Duval*: Marlene Dietrich; *Johnny Marshall*: George Raft; *Jumbo Wells*: Alan Hale; *Omaha*: Frank McHugh; *Dolly*: Eve Arden.

Director: Raoul Walsh; *Producer*: Mark Hellinger; *Executive Producer*: Hal B. Wallis; *Photographer*: Ernest Haller; *Music*: Adolph Deutsch; *Art Director*: Max Parker; *Costumes*: Milo Anderson; *Musical Director*: Leo F. Forbstein; *Editor*: Ralph Dawson; *Sound*: Dolph Thomas; *Special Effects*: Byron Haskin, H. F. Koenekamp; *Makeup*: Perc Westmore; *Original Screenplay*: Richard Macaulay, Jerry Wald; *Songs*: "I'm in No Mood for Music Tonight"; "He lied and I Listened" *by* Frederick Hollander *and* Frank Loesser.

THE LADY IS WILLING
(Columbia, 1942)

Elizabeth Madden: Marlene Dietrich; *Dr Corey McBain*: Fred MacMurray; *Buddy*: Aline MacMahon.

Director and Producer: Mitchell Leisen; *Script*: James Edward Grant, Albert McCleery; *Photographer*: Ted Tetzlaff; *Music*: W. Franke Harling; *Supervising Art Director*: Lionel Banks; *Art Director*: Rudolph Sternad; *Editor*: Eda Warren; *Sound*: Lodge Cunningham; *Dance Director*: Douglas Dean; *Musical Director*: Morris Stoloff; *Song*: "Strange Thing (And I Find You)" *by* Jack King *and* Gordon Clifford.

THE SPOILERS
(Universal, 1942)

Cherry Mallotte: Marlene Dietrich; *Alex McNamara*: Randolph Scott; *Roy Glennister*: John Wayne; *Helen Chester*: Margaret Lindsay; *Dextry*: Harry Carey; *Bronco Kid*: Richard Barthelmess.

Director: Ray Enright; *Producer*: Frank Lloyd; *Script*: Lawrence Hazard, Tom Reed; *Photographer*: Milton Krasner; *Editor*: Clarence Kolster; *Music*: Hans J. Salter; *Musical Director*: Charles Previn; *Costumes*: Vera West; *Art Directors*: Jack Otterson,

John B. Goodman; *Sets*: Russell A. Gausman, Edward R. Robinson; *Sound*: Bernard B. Brown.

PITTSBURGH
(Universal, 1942)

Josie Winters: Marlene Dietrich; *Cash Evans*: Randolph Scott; *Pittsburgh Markham*: John Wayne.

Director: Lewis Seiler; *Producer*: Charles K. Feldman; *Script*: Kenneth Gamet, Tom Reed; *Additional Dialogue*: John Twist; *Photographer*: Robert de Grasse; *Music*: Frank Skinner, Hans J. Salter; *Costumes*: Vera West; *Art Director*: John B. Goodman; *Musical Director*: Charles Previn; *Editor*: Paul Landres; *Special Effects*: John P. Fulton.

FOLLOW THE BOYS
(Universal, 1944)

Tony West: George Raft; *Gloria Vance*: Vera Zorina; *Kitty West*: Grace McDonald; *Nick West*: Charley Grapewin; *Louie Fairweather*: Charles Butterworth. *As themselves*: Jeanette MacDonald, Orson Welles' Mercury Wonder Show, Marlene Dietrich, Dinah Shore, Donald O'Connor, Peggy Ryan, W. C. Fields, The Andrew Sisters, Artur Rubinstein, Sophie Tucker, Maria Montez, Lon Chaney, Jr., Andy Devine, Turhan Bey.

Director: Eddie Sutherland; *Producer*: Charles K. Feldman; *Photographer*: David Abel; *Dance*: George Hale; *Art Directors*: John B. Goodman, Harold H. MacArthur; *Musical Director*: Leigh Harline; *Editor*: Fred R. Reitshaus, Jr.; *Costumes*: Vera West; *Sound*: Bernard B. Brown; *Original Screenplay*: Lou Breslow, Gertrude Purcell.

KISMET
(MGM, 1944)

Hafiz: Ronald Colman; *Jamilla*: Marlene Dietrich; *Caliph*: James Craig; *Mansur*: Edward Arnold.

Director: William Dieterle; *Producer*: Everett Riskin; *Script*: John Meehan; *Photographer*: Charles Rosher; *Music*: Herbert Stothart; *Art Directors*: Cedric Gibbons, Daniel B. Cathcart; *Sound*: Douglas Shearer; *Editor*: Ben Lewis; *Costumes*: Irene, *executed by* Karinska; *Songs*: "Willow in the Wind"; "Tell Me, Tell Me, Evening Star" *by* Harold Arlen *and* E. Y. Harburg.

MARTIN ROUMAGNAC
(Alcina, 1946)

Blanche Ferrand: Marlene Dietrich; *Martin Roumagnac*: Jean Gabin; *Martin's sister*: Margo Lion.

Director: Georges Lacombe; *Producer*: Marc le Pelletier; *Script*: Pierre Very; *Photographer*: Robert Hubert; *Art Director*: George Wakhevitch; *Music*: Marcel Mirouze.

GOLDEN EARRINGS
(Paramount, 1947)

Colonel Ralph Denistoun: Ray Milland; *Lydia*: Marlene Dietrich; *Zoltan*: Murvyn Vye; *Byrd*: Bruce Lester; *Hoff*: Dennis Hoey; *Himself*: Quentin Reynolds; *Professor Krosigk*: Reinhold Schünzel.

Director: Mitchell Leisen; *Producer*: Harry Tugend; *Script*: Abraham Polonsky, Frank Butler, Helen Deutsch; *Photographer*: Daniel L. Fapp; *Art Directors*: Hans Dreier, John Meehan; *Special Effects*: Gordon Jennings; *Set Directors*: Sam Comer, Grace Gregory; *Music*: Victor Young; *Editor*: Alma Macrorie; *Costumes*: Kay Dodson; *Dance*: Billy Daniels; *Makeup*: Wally Westmore; *Sound*: Don Mckay, Walter Oberst; *Song*: "Golden Earrings" *by* Victor Young, Jay Livingstone *and* Ray Evans.

A FOREIGN AFFAIR
(Paramount, 1948)

Phoebe Frost: Jean Arthur; *Erika von Schluetow*: Marlene Dietrich; *Captain John Pringle*: John Lund; *Colonel Rufus J. Plummer*: Millard Mitchell.

Director: Billy Wilder; *Producer*: Charles Brackett; *Script*: Charles Brackett, Billy Wilder, Richard L. Breen; *Adaptation*: Robert Harari; *Photographer*: Charles B. Lang, Jr.; *Special Effects*: Gordon Jennings; *Editor*: Doane Harrison; *Music*: Frederick Hollander; *Costumes*: Edith Head; *Songs*: "Black Market"; "Illusions"; "Ruins of Berlin" *by* Frederick Hollander.

JIGSAW
(Tower Pictures, released through United Artists, 1949)

Howard Malloy: Franchot Tone; *Barbara Whitfield*: Jean Wallace; *Nightclub entertainer*: Marlene Dietrich; *Nightclub patron*: Fletcher Markle; *Nightclub waiter*: Henry Fonda; *Street loiterer*: John Garfield; *Secretary*: Marsha Hunt; *Columnist*: Leonard Lyons; *Barman*: Burgess Meredith.

Director: Fletcher Markle; *Producers*: Edward J. Danziger, Harry Lee Danziger; *Script*: Fletcher Markle, Vincent McConnor; *Photographer*: Don Malkames; *Music*: Robert W. Stringer; *Editor*: Robert Matthews; *Special Effects*: William L. Nemeth; *Sound*: David M. Polak; *Makeup*: Fred Ryle.

STAGE FRIGHT
(Warner Bros.-First National, 1950)

Eve Gill: Jane Wyman; *Charlotte Inwood*: Marlene Dietrich; *Smith*: Michael Wilding; *Jonathan Cooper*: Richard Todd; *Commodore Gill*: Alistair Sim; *Nellie*: Kay Walsh; *Mrs Gill*: Sybil Thorndike.

Director and Producer: Alfred Hitchcock; *Script*: Whitfield Cook; *Adaptation*: Alma Reville; *Additional Dialogue*: James Bridie; *Photographer*: Wilkie Cooper; *Editor*: Edward Jarvis; *Art Director*: Terence Verity; *Music*: Leighton Lucas; *Jane Wyman's costumes*: Milo Anderson; *Marlene Dietrich's costumes*: Christian Dior; *Sound*: Harold King.

NO HIGHWAY IN THE SKY
(20th Century-Fox, 1951)

Mr Honey: James Stewart; *Monica Teasdale*: Marlene Dietrich; *Marjorie Corder*: Glynis Johns; *Dennis Scott*: Jack Hawkins; *Sir John*: Ronald Squire; *Elspeth Honey*: Janette Scott.

Director: Henry Koster; *Producer*: Louis D. Lighton; *Script*: R. C. Sherriff, Oscar Millard, Alec Coppel; *Photographer*: Georges Perinal; *Editor*: Manuel del Campo; *Art Director*: C. P. Norman; *Sound*: Buster Ambler; *Marlene Dietrich's costumes*: Christian Dior.

RANCHO NOTORIOUS
(Fidelity Pictures, distributed by RKO-Radio Pictures, 1952)

Altar Keane: Marlene Dietrich; *Vern Haskell*: Arthur Kennedy; *Frenchy Fermont*: Mel Ferrer.

Director: Fritz Lang; *Producer*: Howard Welsch; *Script*: Daniel Taradash; *Photographer*: Hal Mohr; *Editor*: Otto Ludwig; *Production Designer*: Wiard Ihnen; *Set Decorator*: Robert Priestley; *Marlene Dietrich's costumes by* Don Loper; *Costumes*: Joe King; *Music*: Emil Newman; *Technicolor Color Consultant*: Richard Mueller; *Sound*: Hugh McDowell, Mac Dalgeish; *Makeup*: Frank Westmore; *Songs*: "Gypsy Davey"; "Get Away, Young Man"; "Legend of Chuck-a-Luck" *by* Ken Darby.

AROUND THE WORLD IN 80 DAYS
(Michael Todd Company, Inc., released through United Artists, 1956)

Phileas Fogg: David Niven; *Passepartout*: Cantinflas; *Mr Fix*: Robert Newton; *Aouda*: Shirley MacLaine; *with* Charles Boyer, Joe E. Brown, Martine Carol, John Carradine, Charles Coburn, Ronald Colman, Melville Cooper, Noël Coward, Finlay Currie, Reginald Denny, Andy Devine, Marlene Dietrich, Luis Miguel Dominguin, Fernandel, John Gielgud, Hermione Gingold, Jose Greco, Cedric Hardwicke, Trevor Howard, Glynis Johns, Buster Keaton, Evelyn Keyes, Beatrice Lillie, Peter Lorre, Edmund Lowe, Victor McLaglen, Colonel Tim McCoy, A. E. Matthews, Mike Mazurki, John Mills, Alan Mowbray, Robert Morley, Edward R. Murrow, Jack Oakie, George Raft, Gilbert Roland, Cesar Romero, Frank Sinatra, Red Skelton, Ronald Squire, Basil Sydney, Richard Wattis *and* Harcourt Williams.

Director: Michael Anderson; *Producer*: Michael Todd; *Associate Producer*: William Cameron Menzies; *Script*: S. J. Perelman, James Poe, John Farrow; *Music*: Victor Young; *Costumes*: Miles White; *Photographer*: Lionel Lindon; *Editors*: Gene Ruggiero, Paul Weatherwax; *Art Directors*: James W. Sullivan, Ken Adam.

THE MONTE CARLO STORY
(Titanus Production, released through United Artists, 1957)

Marquise Maria de Crevecoeur: Marlene Dietrich; *Count Dino della Fiaba*: Vittorio de Sica; *Mr Hinkley*: Arthur O'Connell; *Jane Hinkley*: Natalie Trundy.

Director: Samuel A. Taylor; *Producer*: Marcello Girosi; *Script*: Samuel A. Taylor; *Photographer*: Giuseppe Rotunno; *Production Manager*: Nino Misiano; *Art Director*: Gastone Medin; *Sound*: Kurt Dobrawsky; *Costumes*: Elio Costanzi; *Songs*: "Les jeux Sont Faits"; "Rien ne Va Plus"; "Back Home in Indiana" *by* Michael Emer.

WITNESS FOR THE PROSECUTION
(Edward Small-Arthur Hornblow Production, released through United Artists, 1958)

Leonard Vole: Tyrone Power; *Christine Vole*: Marlene Dietrich; *Sir Wilfrid Robarts*: Charles Laughton; *Miss Plimsoll*: Elsa Lanchester; *Brogan-Moore*: John Williams; *Mayhew*: Henry Daniell.

Director: Billy Wilder; Producer: Arthur Hornblow, Jr.; Script: Billy Wilder, Harry Kurnitz; Adaptation: Larry Marcus; Photographer: Russell Harlan; Marlene Dietrich's costumes: Edith Head; Costumes: Joseph King; Makeup: Ray Sebastian, Harry Ray, Gustaf Norin; Editor: Daniel Mandell; Sets: Howard Bristol; Art Director: Alexander Trauner; Music: Matty Malneck; Sound: Fred Lau and Samuel Goldwyn Sound Department; Song: "I May Never Go Home Anymore" by Ralph Arthur Roberts and Jack Brooks.

TOUCH OF EVIL
(Universal-International, 1958)

Ramon Miguel Vargas: Charlton Heston; Susan Vargas: Janet Leigh; Hank Quinlan: Orson Welles; Pete/Menzies: Joseph Calleia; "Uncle" Joe Grandi: Akim Tamiroff; with Marlene Dietrich, Zsa Zsa Gabor, Mercedes McCambridge, Joseph Cotten.

Director: Orson Welles; Producer: Albert Zugsmith; Script: Orson Welles; Costumes: Bill Thomas; Music: Henry Mancini; Assistant Director: Phil Bowles; Photographer: Russell Metty.

JUDGMENT AT NUREMBERG
(Roxlom Production, released through United Artists, 1961)

Judge Dan Haywood: Spencer Tracy; Ernst Janning: Burt Lancaster; Colonel Tad Lawson: Richard Widmark; Mme. Bertholt: Marlene Dietrich; Hans Rolfe: Maximilian Schell; Irene Hoffman: Judy Garland; Rudolf Peterson: Montgomery Clift.

Director and Producer: Stanley Kramer; Associate Producer: Philip Langner; Script: Abby Mann; Photographer: Ernest Laszlio; Editor: Fred Knudtson; Music: Ernest Gold; Production Designer and Art Director: Rudolph Sternad; Costumes: Jean Louis, Joseph King; Sets: George Milo.

THE BLACK FOX
(Arthur Steloff-Image Production, released by Heritage Films, Inc., 1962)

Director and Producer: Louis Clyde Stoumen; Executive Producer: Jack le Vien; Script: Louis Clyde Stoumen; Narrator: Marlene Dietrich; Animation Supervision: Al Stahl; Editors: Kenn Collins, Mark Wortreich; Music: Ezra Laderman; Distributed by MGM.

PARIS WHEN IT SIZZLES
(Paramount, 1964)

Richard Benson: William Holden; Gabrielle Simpson: Audrey Hepburn; Police Inspector: Gregoire Aslan; Alexander Mayerheimer: Noël Coward; with Marlene Dietrich, Tony Curtis, Mel Ferrer, and the voices of Fred Astaire and Frank Sinatra.

Director: Richard Quine; Producers: Richard Quine, George Axelrod; Script: George Axelrod; Photographer: Charles Lang, Jr.; Music: Nelson Riddle; Sets: Jean d'Eauboune; Audrey Hepburn's costumes: Hubert de Givenchy; Marlene Dietrich's costumes: Christian Dior; Editor: Archie Marshek.

JUST A GIGOLO
(Leguan, 1978)

Paul von Prsygodsky: David Bowie; Cilly: Sydne Rome; Helga: Kim Novak; Captain Hermann Kraft: David Hemmings; Mutti: Maria Schell; Prince: Curd Jurgens; Baroness von Semering: Marlene Dietrich.

Director: David Hemmings; Producer: Rolf Thiele; Script: Ennio de Concini, Joshua Sinclair; Photographer: Charly Steinberger; Editor: Alfred Srp; Production Designer: Peter Rothe; Music: Günther Fischer; Costumes: Max Maga, Ingrid Zore; Choreographer: Herbert F. Schubert; Sound: Günther Kortwich; Songs: "Revolutionary Song" by David Bowie and Jack Fishman; "Jonny" by Frederick Hollander and Jack Fishman; "I Kiss Your Hand, Madame" by Ralph Erwin, Fritz Rotter and Sam Lewis; "Just a Gigolo" by L. Casucci and Irving Caesar; "Don't Let It Be Too Long" by Gunther Fischer and David Hemmings.

BIBLIOGRAPHY

Books

The Films of Marlene Dietrich, by Homer Dickens (Citadel, Secaucus, New Jersey, revised edition, 1980). Filmography with credits and selected review quotations; contains interesting material on Dietrich's German period.

Fun in a Chinese Laundry, by Josef von Sternberg (The Macmillan Co., New York; Secker and Warburg, London, 1965). Idiosyncratic account by Dietrich's mentor of his relationship with her.

Marlene Dietrich, by John Kobal (Dutton, New York; Studio Vista, London, 1968). A brief but well-illustrated study.

Marlene, by Charles Higham (Granada, London, 1978). A life, gossipy in parts, but containing interesting first-hand interviews with some of Dietrich's (now deceased) contemporaries.

Four Fabulous Faces, by Larry Carr (Galahad, New York, 1970). Lushly illustrated picture album of Dietrich and three contemporaries (Garbo, Crawford, Swanson), with perceptive commentary.

Marlene Dietrich, by Sheridan Morley (Elm Tree, London, 1976). A compact study, especially good in evoking Dietrich the diseuse.

Articles in Magazines and Periodicals

Picturegoer, May 1931: article on early life; Picturegoer, November 7, 14, 21, 1931: three-part article on life and career to date; Photoplay, February 1932, November 1941: parody and career speculation respectively; Films in Review, December 1954, May 1968, January 1971: career articles with filmographies; Positif, No. 75, 1966: series of articles (in French) about various aspects of Dietrich's career, with particular attention to her relationship with Von Sternberg; Mein Film, August 6, 13, 20, 1954: three-part career article (in German); Berlin Film Festival, 1977, 1978: selective reprints of contemporary reviews and articles to accompany a two-part Dietrich retrospective. See also Notes on the Text for further periodical sources.

NOTES ON THE TEXT

1 Dietrich, quoted by Charles Graves, *Daily Sketch*, December 24, 1936.

2 Dietrich, quoted by Stefan Lorant, *News Chronicle*, October 1, 1935.

3 Peter Panter, *Die Weltbühne*, October 25, 1923.

4 Kurt Tucholsky, *Gesammelte Werke*, Vol. 1: 1907–1924 (Reinbek, 1960)

5 Heinz Herald, quoted in *The Haunted Screen*, by Lotte H. Eisner (Thames and Hudson, London, 1969), p. 177.

6 Roland Schacht, *B.Z.am Mittag*, November 8, 1923.

7 Hans Feld, *Berliner Börsen-Courier*, January 26, 1927.

8 Hans Sahl, *Der Montag Morgen*, January 21, 1929.

9 Anon., *Hamburger Anzeiger*, January 24, 1929.

10 Hanns G. Lustig, *Tempo*, January 18, 1929.

11 Manfred George, quoted in *Positif*, No. 75, 1966.

12 Hans Sahl, *Der Montag Morgen*, September 23, 1929.

13 Robin Irvine, *Film Weekly*, March 28, 1931.

14 "G.F.," *Neue Zeitung*, Munich, April 15, 1930.

15 Lotte H. Eisner, *Film-Kurier*, Berlin, July 22, 1930.

16 *Fun in a Chinese Laundry*, by Josef von Sternberg (The Macmillan Co., New York; Secker and Warburg, London, 1965), p. 227.

17 Ibid., p. 232.

18 *Marlene Dietrich*, by John Kobal (Dutton, New York; Studio Vista, London, 1968) p. 44.

19 Friedrich Hussong Neuland, *Der Montag*, March 31, 1930.

20 Herbert Ihering, *Berliner Börsen-Courier*, April 2, 1930.

21 Wolf Zucker, *Die literarische Welt*, April 11, 1930.

22 Hans Sahl, *Der Montag Morgen*, April 7, 1930.

23 Stefan Lorant, *op. cit.* (note 2).

24 *A Private View*, by Irene Mayer Selznick (Weidenfeld and Nicolson, London, 1983), p. 136.

25 Sam Jaffe, conversation with the author, September 19, 1983.

26 Dietrich, quoted by Peter Bogdanovich, *Esquire*, October 1973.

27 *The Cinema of Josef von Sternberg*, by John Baxter (Barnes, New York; Zwemmer, London, 1971), p. 90.

28 Dietrich, quoted in the London *Evening Standard*, March 29, 1931.

29 Maria Riva, quoted by Selma Robinson, *Ladies Home Journal*, October, 1951.

30 Dietrich, quoted in *Film Weekly*, March, 1932.

31 "A.D.S." (André Sennwald), *The New York Times*, September 15, 1934.

32 Richard Watts Jr., *New York Herald Tribune*, September 14, 1934.

33 Dietrich, quoted in *Films and Filming*, June, 1963.

34 Frank Nugent, *The New York Times*, April 13, 1936.

35 Charles Graves, *Daily Sketch*, December 24, 1936.

36 *Memo from David O. Selznick*, ed. by Rudy Behlmer (Macmillan, London, 1972), p. 99.

37 Ibid., p. 103.

38 "Marlene Dietrich, Kodachrome Moviemaker," by William Stull ASC, *American Cinematographer*, May, 1941.

39 Charles Graves, *op. cit.*, December 23, 1936.

40 Dietrich, quoted in *Picturegoer*, August 22, 1936.

41 Dietrich, quoted in the London *Evening Standard*, January 4, 1936.

42 Frank Nugent, *The New York Times*, November 4, 1937.

43 *Mitchell Leisen*, by David Chierichetti (Curtis, New York, 1973), pp. 175–6.

44 "Welcome, Marlene," by Leo Lerman, *Vogue*, August 15, 1944.

45 *Marlene Dietrich*, by Sheridan Morley (Elm Tree, London, 1976), p. 98.

46 Ibid., p. 100.

47 Dick Williams, New York *Mirror*, December 17, 1953.

48 Dietrich, quoted by Art Buchwald, *Sunday Chronicle*, July 17, 1955.

49 Milo Anderson, quoted in *Los Angeles Times*, August 19, 1983.

50 Jack Kroll, *Newsweek*, October 23, 1967.

51 Peter Bogdanovich, *Esquire*, October 1973.

52 Dietrich, quoted by John Francis Lane, *Films and Filming*, December, 1956.

53 Dietrich, quoted by Rex Reed, *Los Angeles Times*, January 8, 1973.

SOURCES OF ILLUSTRATIONS

Except for those illustrations noted below, all pictorial material comes from the archives of the Kobal Collection, London. Mr John Kobal wishes to acknowledge with thanks the help of Ms Mary Corliss of the Museum of Modern Art, New York; Ms Helge Bellach and Mr Peter Magdowski of the Stiftung Deutsche Kinemathek, Berlin; Ms Micky Glassge of the Deutsches Institut für Filmkunde, Frankfurt; and Ms Juliet Benita Colman.

Culver Pictures: page 74 (below).
London Films: page 140.
Magnum Photos: photo by Erich Salomon, page 78 (above); photos by Eve Arnold, pages 159, 191 (below).
Paris Match: photo by François Gragnon, page 197.
Phototeque: page 148 (below).
Ullstein Bilderdienst: pages 14, 21, 30, 184–5, 186 (above).

Page numbers in *italic* refer to the illustrations